Black Crosses
off my
Wingtip

Squadron Leader I. F. Kennedy DFC & Bar

GSPH

Published by

GENERAL STORE
PUBLISHING HOUSE

1 Main Street Burnstown, Ontario, Canada K0J 1G0
Telephone (613) 432-7697 or (613) 432-9385

ISBN 0-919431-82-8
Printed and Bound in Canada.

Layout and Design by Mervin Price
Cover Design by Leanne Enright

General Store Publishing House gratefully acknowledges the assistance
of the Ontario Arts Council.

Canadian Cataloguing in Publication Data

Kennedy, Irving Farmer, 1922 -
Black crosses off my wingtip

Includes bibliographical references
ISBN 0-919431-82-8

Cover Painting by R.W. Bradford, National Air Museum

1. Kennedy, Irving Farmer, 1922 - . 2. World War, 1939-1945
– Personal narratives, Canadian. 3. Canada. Royal Canadian Air Force
– Biography. 4. Air pilots, Military –Canada – Biography. I. Title.

D811.K38 1994   940.54'4971'0971   C94-900140-6

First Printing February 1994

This book is dedicated to my brother
and all those light-hearted young
lads whom we knew only a little
while, who laughed and flew, but
did not come home again.
We never had a chance to say
good-bye . . .

Acknowledgement

I must confess that, without the girls, I would never have told this story.
They thought that there was a tale hidden in the recesses of four and a
half years of war.
If it has any merit, therefore, credit must go to my sister Joyce, my
wife Fern, and my daughters Ann and Carol, who persuaded and
encouraged, criticized and typed, - when I was unsure.
I thank them all.

Contents

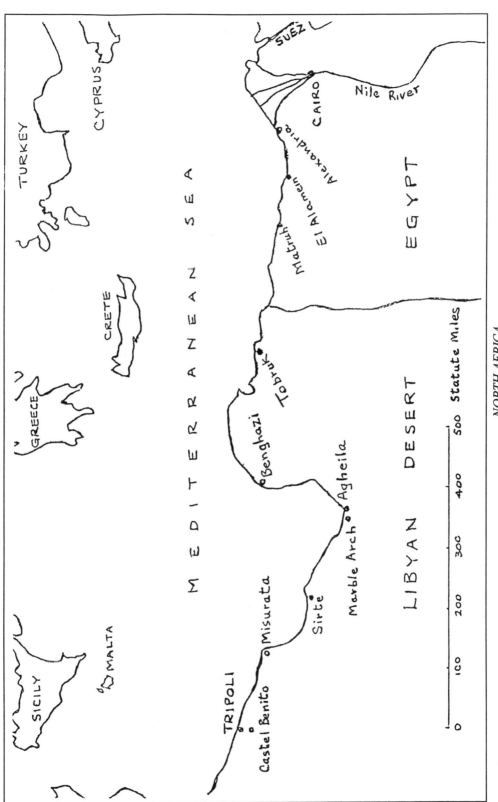

NORTH AFRICA

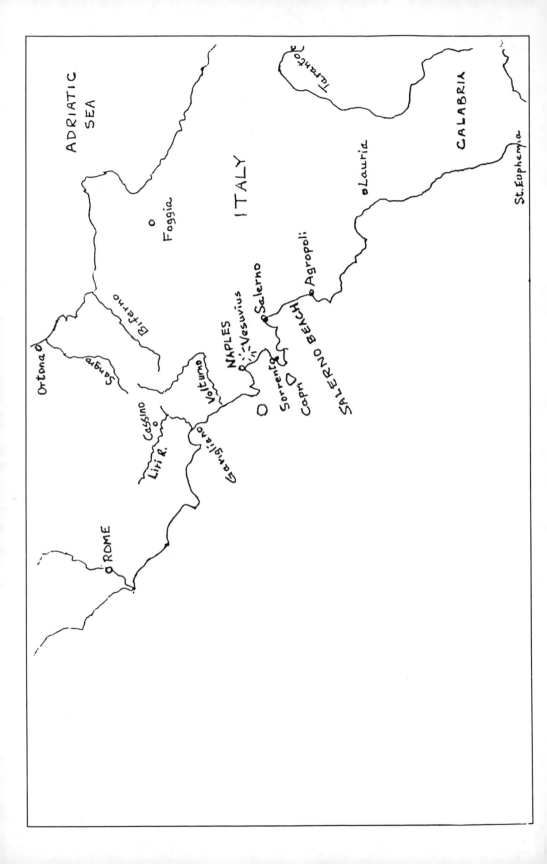

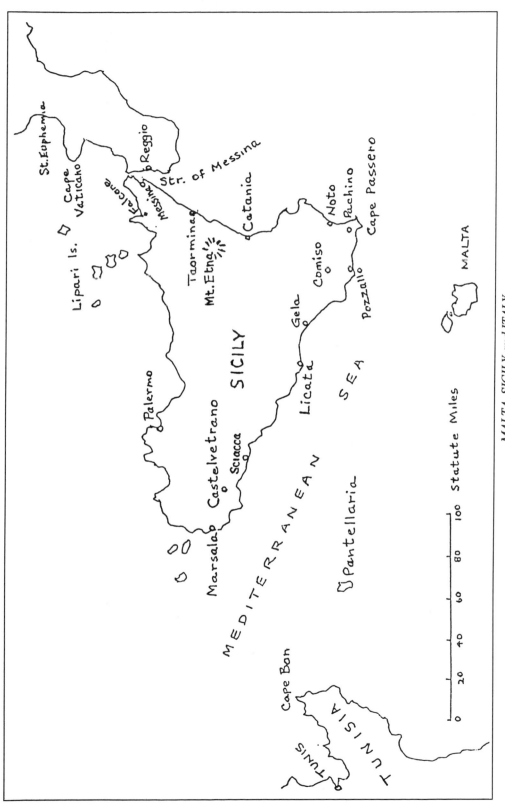

MALTA, SICILY and ITALY

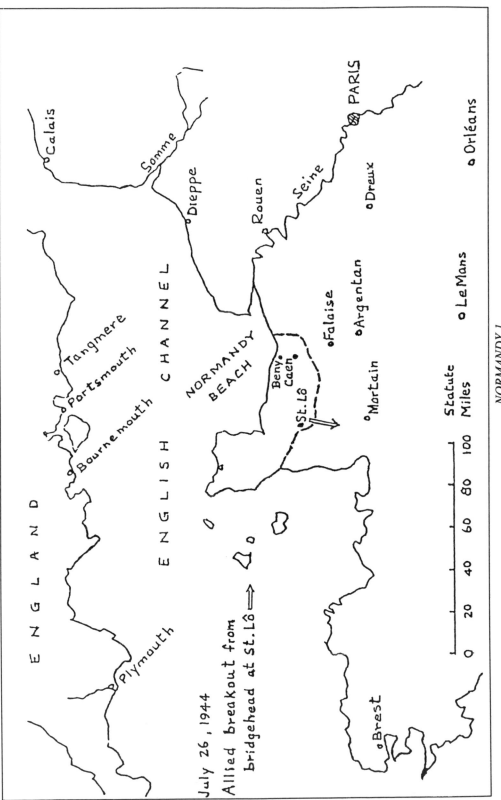

July 26, 1944
Allied breakout from
bridgehead at St. Lô

NORMANDY 1

NORMANDY 2

Whirlwind twin-engined fighter. The Author flew this aircraft (P7110) in 263 Squadron, RAF, in 1941.

263 SQDN. RAF 1941-42

Front Row: Jim Coyne RCAF, Mick Muirhead RCAF (KIFA), Ken Ridley, Johnnie Walker (KIA), Sam Small, Stu Lovell, Ceylon; Bill Lovell USA, RCAF (KIA).

Second Row: Eddie Brearley RCAF (KIA), Joe Holmes, Norm Crabtree USA; Sqdn. Ldr. Tom Pugh, Ireland (KIA), G/C Harvey, Station C.O.; Geoff Warnes (KIA), E.C. Owens, Adjutant; Tim Harvey (KIA), Blackie Blackshaw (KIA).

Third Row: O.E. Hay, Engineering Officer; Peter Ewing RAAF (KIA), Les Currie, N. Ireland (KIA), Peter Brannigan RNZAF, Rex King, Trinidad (KIA), Don Gill RCAF (KIA), Colin Bell RAAF (KIA).

Back Row: Dick Reed USA, RCAF, Basil Abrams S. Africa (KIA), Hap Kennedy RCAF, Peter Jardine S. Africa (KIFA), Roy Wright.

(KIA = Killed in action. KIFA=Killed in flying accident. Pilots are British unless otherwise indicated.)

Spitfire in a steep turn, the most important manoeuvre in combat.
Note the ailerons holding the vertical turn.
(Photo courtesy AVM J. E. Johnson. C.B,C.B.E., DSO., DFC.)

Messerschmitt Bf 109G, a formidable opponent.
(Photo by John Dibbs via John Elcome, Bf 109G Restoration.)

A Spitfire pilot in England, 1942.

BLACK CROSSES OFF MY WINGTIP
Introduction

It is with some reluctance that I have recounted this war story. Wars are neither pretty nor petty, but they don't pretend to be. They have been, I think, the essence of history. And as we were young men in late 1939 when the Second World War began, we inevitably became involved in that most serious conflict.

My reluctance is very basic: I have no wish to stir up old animosity. It was, of course, absolutely impossible to become actively involved in the fighting without experiencing animosity, and my story will reflect that feeling.

On the other hand, I have sometimes felt that I should tell what it was like, flying with a fighter squadron, on behalf of many of my comrades who died very young and who were unable to speak for themselves. This latter sentiment has prevailed. I have mentioned a few of those lads; I remember them all.

I hope, therefore, that my story is reasonable, – or as close to reason as war allows.

This is the true story of a Spitfire pilot's experiences. I did not keep a tedious diary; however, notes of significant happenings, my Pilot's Flying Log Book, and concise Combat Reports have provided the places, squadrons, names, dates, times and even the weather of events. Coordinating my notes, logbook and combat reports with reference to Second World War histories by John Keegan, and by Desmond Flower and James Reeves, has been a delight; verifying my combat reports with air war historian Christopher Shores has proven most gratifying; while in the prologue I have referred to Norman Rich's fine history of Hitler's war aims.

My early impatient days in the Royal Canadian Air Force were only a means to an end. I learned to fly in western Canada, got my "wings" on June 21, 1941 (the day before Germany invaded Russia) and proceeded at once via troopship to Britain. Following six weeks of operational training on Hurricanes that had survived the Battle of Britain, I arrived at an RAF fighter squadron in September.

My first fourteen months, nine on Whirlwinds and five on Spitfires, were not consistently exciting, but there were some interesting sweeps across the channel to France. I learned a bit about survival which stood me in good stead when, in late 1942, I arrived in Malta, where this story of deep friendships and indelible actions begins.

I.F.K.

Prologue
WHAT HAD GONE BEFORE

On the Origin of War:

It is tempting to close one's eyes to history, and instead to speculate about the roots of war in some possible animal instinct . . . But war, organized war is not a human instinct. It is a highly planned and cooperative form of theft. And that form of theft began ten thousand years ago when the harvesters of wheat accumulated a surplus, and the nomads rose out of the desert to rob them of what they themselves could not provide. The evidence of that [is] in the walled city of Jericho and its prehistoric tower. That is the beginning of war.

J. Bronowski in The Ascent of Man

On Nazi Philosophy:

The folkish philosophy finds the importance of mankind in its basic racial elements . . . Thus it by no means believes in an equality of the races, but . . . recognizes their higher or lesser value and feels itself obligated . . . to promote the victory of the better and stronger, and demand the subordination of the inferior and weaker [race] . . .

Human culture and civilization on this continent [Europe] are inseparably bound up with the presence of the Aryan . . . And so the folkish philosophy . . . must lead to a continuous mutual higher breeding, until . . . the best of humanity, having achieved possession of this earth, will have a free path for activity . . .

In the distant future humanity must be faced by problems which only a highest race, become master people . . . will be equipped to overcome . . . This is the goal pursued by the National Socialist German Workers' Party.

Adolf Hitler in Mein Kampf

Pre-War Annexations of Austria and Czechoslovakia

[Hitler reasoned that] in order to wage war against the Western powers, it would be an enormous advantage to have Austria and Czechoslovakia eliminated beforehand . . .

On March 12, 1938, German troops marched unopposed over the Austrian border. The era of Nazi territorial expansion had begun . . .

Hitler . . . demanded the return to the Reich of the three million Germans in Czechoslovakia . . . At his invitation the leaders of the British, French and Italian governments met in Munich, where . . . the conference on September 29, 1938, met all Hitler's demands . . . [i.e.] the German annexation of the Sudetenland . . . Still Hitler was not satisfied and in March 1939 he undertook the final liquidation of the Czechoslovak state.

Norman Rich in Hitler's War Aims

The Second World War Begins

August 22, 1939: Hitler reviewed the international and military situation with his supreme commanders . . . The elimination of Poland was an essential precondition to a western campaign . . .

[Hitler said:] "When starting and waging a war it is not right that matters, but victory. Close your hearts to pity. Act brutally. Eighty million people must obtain what is their right . . . The wholesale destruction of Poland is the military objective . . . Complete annihilation . . . "

[Although Hitler knew that Britain and France had treaties of mutual assistance with Poland,] on September 1, 1939, German troops crossed the Polish frontier . . . On that day the British and French governments demanded that Germany suspend its aggressive action against Poland, otherwise they would fulfil their military obligations to that country. The Germans . . . did not suspend their activities, and on September 3 Britain and France declared war on Germany. The second world war had begun . . . Within four weeks all effective Polish resistance had been broken.

On September 28 Russia and Germany signed a treaty dividing Poland between them. Hitler was now free to deal with his opponents to the west.

Norman Rich in Hitler's War Aims

The Conquest of Europe: Hitler Turns West

November 3, 1939. Adolf Hitler to the German High Command: "I did not organize the Armed Forces in order not to strike. The decision to strike was always in me . . . I shall attack France and England at the most favourable and earliest moment. Breach of the neutrality of Belgium and Holland is meaningless. No one will question that when we have won."

Flower and Reeves in The War 1939-1945

April 9, 1940: German forces attacked and occupied Denmark and Norway, overwhelming valiant Norwegian resistance in three weeks.

May 10, 1940: German forces invaded the Netherlands (bombing Rotterdam), Belgium and Luxembourg WITHOUT a declaration of war. The German blitzkrieg of these three countries was over on May 27th.

The Fall of France:

May 13, 1940: German forces invaded France. The superior German armour overwhelmed the French Army and by the end of the month had driven the British Expeditionary Force back to the French coast at Dunkirk, from which they were evacuated to Britain. The French and British troops were incapable of stopping the German Panzer divisions. Marshal Pétain considered the defeat of France the prelude to the collapse of all of Europe.

June 22, 1940: Hitler insisted that the armistice with France be signed in the forest of Compiègne in the same railway car that had been used for signing the German capitulation on November 11, 1918.

June 18, 1940: After the fall of France, [General] Charles de Gaulle . . . determined to carry on resistance . . . broadcast from London to the French people: "This war has not been settled by the Battle of France. This war is a world war . . . whatever happens the flame of resistance must not and will not be extinguished." He called on all Frenchmen who could join him on British soil to continue the fight.

John Keegan in The Second World War

The Determination of Winston Churchill

June 18, 1940: "The Battle of France is over. I expect that the Battle of Britain is about to begin . . . The whole fury and might of the enemy must very soon be turned on us. Hitler knows that he will have to break us in this island or lose the war. If we can stand up to him, all Europe may be free and the life of the world may move forward into broad sunlit uplands. But if we fail, then the whole world, including the United States, including all that we have known and cared for, will sink into the abyss of a new dark age . . . Let us therefore brace ourselves to our duties . . . "

Winston Churchill, Flower and Reeves The War 1939-1945

The Question:

June 1940: "My Luftwaffe is invincible. And so now we turn to England. How long will this one last - two, three weeks?"

Reichsmarschall Hermann Goering, Commander in Chief of the Luftwaffe.

The Answer:

July 1940: "Royal Air Force Fighter Command's men and machines will decide whether or not Hitler comes to London."

Winston Churchill, Prime Minister of Great Britain.

The Battle of Britain:

After the fall of France Hitler returned to Berlin, where on July 6, 1940 he acknowledged the massive cheering crowds from the balcony of the Reichs-chancelry.

Ten days later he issued a Directive on his next move:the English air force must be eliminated prior to "Operation Sealion", the invasion of Great Britain. While landing barges assembled in French ports, the Battle of Britan began.

The Luftwaffe attacks on airfields, ground installations and radar stations in August and early September averaged 1000 aircraft sorties per day. On August 15 the Luftwaffe flew 2199 sorties and lost 75 aircraft while the RAF lost 30 Hurricane and Spitfire fighters. By September 7 both air forces were hurting badly. The RAF's supply of fighter pilots was running out: each squadron averaged only sixteen operational pilots out of their full complement of twenty-six. German aircrew and aircraft losses were heavier but they had more reserves.

At the moment when the battle was in the balance Hitler's patience broke. He ordered the Luftwaffe attack to be diverted from RAF airfields to the cities, in particular toward the demoralization of the people of London. This tactical error allowed the RAF fighter squadrons to rebound with a climactic victory on September 15.

Historian John Keegan wrote: "Hopes that Britain's resistance could be broken while the invading season held collapsed: on 17 September Hitler announced the postponement of Operation Sealion [the invasion of Britain] until further notice . . .

"The victory of 'the Few' was narrow . . . [544 RAF fighter pilots were killed, but Air Chief Marshal Dowding's] Fighter Command . . . inflicted on Nazi Germany its first defeat. The legacy of that defeat would be long delayed in its effects; but the survival of an independent Britain which it assured was the event that most certainly determined the downfall of Hitler's Germany."

John Keegan in The Second World War

Mein Kampf Exemplified:

Nazi ideology as expounded in Mein Kampf demanded the conquest of Russia and the destruction of Bolshevism . . . The collapse of Russia would be the most powerful substantiation of the correctness of what Hitler called the folk theory of race . . .

By the end of 1940 all prospects for a quick . . . defeat of Britain were at an end, and at approximately the same time Hitler . . . made the . . . decision to attack Russia.

Norman Rich in Hitler's War Aims

Hitler Invades Russia:

The Wehrmacht was ready in six months, and on June 22, 1941, three million German troops invaded Russia. Bombs were already falling when the German Ambassador to the U.S.S.R., Count von Schulenburg, handed Soviet Foreign Minister Molotov a note stating that their countries were at war.

The Japanese Attack Pearl Harbour Dec. 7, 1941:

At 7 a.m. about 200 miles north of Hawaii six Japanese aircraft carriers commenced launching 360 aircraft in a surprise attack on the U.S. Navy at Pearl Harbour. This devastating attack destroyed or severely damaged all of the capital ships in harbour.

It was 2 p.m. in Washington when the Japanese Ambassador Nomura arrived at the office of the U.S. Secretary of State, Cordell Hull, and handed him a long diatribe from Tojo. The Secretary, who had just been informed a few minutes earlier of the bombing of Pearl Harbour, showed the Ambassador the door. Thus a state of war existed with Japan.

It was 6 p.m. on a dark and rainy night at a Royal Air Force station in the south of England. Pilots of 263 Squadron had gathered around the wireless in the mess for the B.B.C. news. We learned that the U.S. Navy, in harbour in Hawaii, had just been bombed and torpedoed. The Japanese had thus come into the war on the side of Germany and Italy, with whom they had a pact. The United States, with all its strength, was suddenly thrust into the war.

Now we truly had a world war. Without doubt, it would be a very long, hard fight. But we were not alarmed: we were relieved. Walking back to my billet that night in the soft rain, I felt a quiet contentment. Quite possibly, Hitler and Tojo had bitten off more than they could chew. It was a great time to be young, confident, and impatient to take on the Luftwaffe.

Chapter I
A Good Day For Huns

(Ref. maps:

1. North Africa

2. Malta, Sicily and Italy)

The war on the North African coast of the Mediterranean continued, Montgomery's Eighth Army against Rommel's Afrikakorps in Libya and Eisenhower's forces against von Arnim in Tunisia. Italians reinforced both German armies. The island of Malta, strategically located midway between Gibraltar and Egypt and only 70 miles from Sicily, was a thorn in the side of Hitler and Mussolini, interfering with their plans for expansion to the Near East. In 1942 they had tried, and failed, to bomb Malta into submission. In early 1943 we continued to harass German and Italian forces in Sicily.

"Would you like to take a section of four aircraft and have a look for a Wellington bomber that went down in the sea last night? They were returning from a raid on Northern Italy. There's a possibility that the crew might be in a dinghy within a hundred miles or so of the island."

"Certainly," I answered. "The visibility is good for a search. And it looks like a good day for Huns. We have a fair chance of running into some enemy aircraft whether we find the Wimpy crew or not."

The Commanding Officer of 249 Squadron, RAF, Krendi, Malta, had politely framed a question, but an affirmative reply was, of course, obligatory. On that sunny Sunday morning in March, 1943, he was relaying an order that he had received from Headquarters for a flight. A Wellington bomber from nearby Luqa aerodrome was four hours overdue, and the crew might still be alive. Now his eyes wrinkled in a smile. He was not given to talk much, and quickly got to the point.

"Take whomever you like with you. I think north-west is your best bet. Keep down below two hundred feet and maintain radio silence. You may avoid detection. Keep an eye open for a Very pistol signal flare. Check the Flight Sergeant for aircraft. The sooner you go, the better. And good luck."

"Very good, sir. We'll get airborne right away."

I saw the "Chiefy", as the chief NCO in charge of keeping the squadron's Spitfires serviceable was affectionately known. Before I could say a word, he advised me that four Spits from "B" Flight, including mine, were fuelled, armed, run-up, and ready to go. The ground crew's grapevine, as usual, was functioning well. "A" Flight was on readiness, and a section had already been scrambled after an unidentified aircraft approaching Malta from the north. So "B" Flight had been given this job.

Since we shared a common pilots' dispersal on this landing strip with 229 Squadron, we knew those boys just as well as our own chaps. We were not as familiar with the other three Malta Spitfire squadrons at Luqa and Halfar, but had occasional radio contact in the air.

I wrote "Tiger Blue Section" on the blackboard in the dispersal, and drew a line under it. Usually the flight commander selected the pilots for a sortie, but we had lost our Flight Lieutenant a day or so earlier. "Tiger" was our squadron's call sign, and the boys were keen to fly. Amongst some irreverent remarks from 229 types was the odd request from a 249 pilot to put his name down. I put down my own name, followed by Bentley, Kelly, and Jack. (After all this time, I can't remember Jack's surname, and maybe that's just as well.) I chose Bentley as my number two because he was quietly keen and competent. Kelly was an excellent pilot who had not had any luck at all, and whose morale required a boost. He needed to fire his guns. Jack had been quite voluble lately about never being airborne at the right time.

As I briefed these three fellows on our sortie, I had a genuine feeling that it was a good day for Huns.

"For three reasons," I continued. "A Wellington is down somewhere and will attract attention if within forty miles of Sicily. Secondly, the weather is just right with about six/tenths cumulus cloud cover, which affords some protection to the enemy. And it is a Sunday morning; the Luftwaffe seem to like flying on Sunday mornings. So I really expect that we'll have some fun this morning," I concluded, "and then Kelly and Jack will have nothing more to complain about."

I tightened up the ties of my Mae West[1] as I walked out to my aircraft and climbed into the cockpit. The mechanics had everything ready. The fitter put my parachute straps over my shoulders, then the aircraft harness. Helmet and gloves, oxygen and radio connections, brakes on, then thumbs up to the rigger. "Contact" and the Merlin engine burst into a crackle, then a steady roar of twelve cylinders straining at the chocks. The sound and the tremor implied potential that always thrilled me. Oil pressure OK. Throttle back quickly. The rigger was looking at me as I waved the chocks away, and I moved out of the protective bay. That peculiar tingling elation that I often experienced taxiing out arrived right on schedule.

"God, I feel good," I thought. "This is the best job in the war."

I could see the other three Spits following me down to the end of the strip. I turned into wind, did a final cockpit check, rolled out onto the strip, and opened full throttle. Hard right rudder to counteract torque, then suddenly airborne and flying smoothly. Gear up, gunsight on, gun button safety off.

---

(1)
> *The Mae West was an inflatable lifejacket, named by RAF pilots after the busty Hollywood blonde of the 1930s.*

I circled the strip and watched Bentley and Kelly take off, but then with some dismay saw Jack taxiing back to his parking bay. "What the hell can be the trouble?" I thought. "Well, no matter. It's too late now. Can't break radio silence. We'll be O.K. with three aircraft."

I waggled my wings and the boys came in, one on each side and a little behind me. We were used to flying this way, an open formation adopted from the Luftwaffe. The advantage was great visual cross-cover of each other's tail while at the same time sufficiently spaced apart that there was no danger of collision. One could concentrate on the most important part of air warfare which was seeing the enemy first.

We settled down north of the island, flying comfortably at a hundred feet above the water on a course of 330 degrees, airspeed about 200 mph to conserve fuel. Habit rendered fractional glances at the instruments adequate; survival demanded that one's eyes be out of the cockpit scanning the skies for aircraft. And today we also had to watch the sea for a dinghy or floating flotsam. The Mediterranean was characteristically calm, unlike the cold, green Atlantic and the English Channel. The morning calm was in our favour for spotting anything on the surface.

After thirty-five minutes and a little more than a hundred miles, I turned to port and moved a few miles to the south. Another ninety degrees to port and we were on a reciprocal south-east course. And still no sign of anything. I didn't mind the radio silence. It was a lovely morning; we had left the clouds behind and were flying in brilliant sunshine. I began to wonder if my earlier optimism had been warranted.

Then I saw it! A twin-engined, low wing, single-tail aircraft coming straight toward us! Or was it going away from us? Impossible to say by the silhouette, but it must be coming toward us or I would have seen it sooner. It's either a Junkers Ju 88 or a Beaufighter, I thought. Very similar profiles at a distance.

"Tiger Blue Section. Blue One here," I broke the silence abruptly. "Aircraft nine o'clock same level. Turning port. Full throttle." I had turned ninety degrees before I finished transmitting.

The aircraft was coming straight toward us very quickly, and how they did not see us and take some evasive action before I pulled up over their left wing, I do not know. They were just not looking. Dreaming. Completely taken by surprise.

The Junkers Ju 88 with a crew of four, a beautiful aircraft with excellent performance, passed under me, grey-blue with big black crosses on the fuselage and wings, and a swastika on the tail. The pilot jammed the throttles open. Both engines belched black smoke, but it was a futile attempt to escape. He had about the same top speed as we did, but neither the acceleration nor the manoeuvrability. We were on him in a flash, and he knew he was in trouble.

I made a left rear quarter attack, carefully pulling my gunsight through his line of flight, and as I got within three hundred yards I picked on the port engine. I pressed the firing button and the effect of my two 20 mm. cannons was devastating. His engine was immediately engulfed in fire. As I accelerated out to port, I was conscious of some clattering hits on my aircraft from the rear gunner. I turned parallel to the Junkers and saw Blue Three, Flight Sergeant Kelly, attacking the 88, firing into the fuselage. The fire was rapidly spreading. There wasn't much time left. The German captain decided that their only chance of survival lay in setting the aircraft down on the sea. He shut down his good engine and kicked the rudder pedals hard, violently yawing one way and then the other, attempting to slow the aircraft. A large orange dinghy was thrown out the emergency exit and danced on the water, but the slick Junkers was still going far too fast to ditch.

Meanwhile, it was obvious that Kelly was absorbing punishment from the rear gunner.

Suddenly, I got very angry. Although I knew that Kelly should have moved out and away from the Junkers, I was annoyed at the rear gunner for shooting at him. Kelly was in great danger of being shot down, and one cannot ditch a Spit! It's all engine and goes straight down. And like the Junkers, if Kelly's Spitfire got hit in the engine, there was no altitude to employ a parachute. Or was my anger at the Junkers crew an inappropriate reaction to the knowledge that Kelly did not have to continue firing at all? The fate of the Junkers had been already sealed by the spreading fire.

Although some pilots denied feeling anger in combat while considering it an impersonal game, I knew that some measure of anger was usually behind my determination to destroy Hitler's aircraft. It was the sight of the black crosses at close range that precipitated that indescribable emotion. Then the primitive defence reaction of mind and body took over. All the rest of life and living was incidental, put on the shelf, while the body tingled. And whenever this personal combat became prolonged and difficult, as often happened with a capable adversary, an element of animal anger ensued. But this was a literate animal who at least tried to understand the process. Hitler had marched across Europe from Brest to Stalingrad. He had shouted "Today Europe, tomorrow the world!"

"Damn you!" I replied, venting my fury on the unfortunate Junkers that carried Hitler's black crosses.

And yet, although I did not admit it at the time or even think about it during the war, I know and well remember feeling relief whenever I saw a Luftwaffe pilot's parachute open. And it was the accepted chivalry of war that we never shot an airman in a parachute, and would rescue him from a dinghy if possible, and even allow a Dornier flying boat to pluck him from the sea and take him home, with the probability of having to face this man again.

The rear gunner of the Ju 88, as was customary of gunners, displayed great courage and continued firing until the Junkers became completely enveloped in flames, and crashed into the sea. There were no survivors. Warrant Officer Bentley wisely chose not to attack.

We returned to Malta without further incident. There was no trace of the Wellington crew, and we landed rather low on fuel. As usual, when the mechanics saw the aircraft landing with the gun patches blown off,[2] they enthusiastically beckoned us into the protective sand-bag bays. They were up on the wing as soon as the prop stopped, big smiles hiding their impatience to learn if their very own aircraft had overcome a German aircraft that day.

Kelly had numerous holes in his Spitfire, but he was exuberant. The young lad from Peterborough, Ontario, had finally shared in the destruction of a German aircraft.

Walking in from my Spitfire I met Jack.
"You really missed it today, Jack," I said. "We had a good scrap. I told you that this was a good day for Huns. What was the problem?"
"My oil pressure was a bit low," Jack replied. "It was a bit below normal."

There seemed to be nothing more to say, and besides, I had to see the Intelligence Officer and complete a combat report. Then I sought out the chief N.C.O. regarding the aircraft.

"What's the oil pressure problem on that Spit that didn't come with us, Chiefy?"
"That's TN," he said, identifying the letters on the Spitfire. "There is no oil pressure problem on that aircraft, sir," Chiefy replied, looking right at me. The Flight Sergeant was, at forty-two years, exactly twice my age, permanent force, and knew that his "sir" sometimes embarrassed a young officer. But there was a serious implication here.

"You're sure?" I asked.
"Absolutely. Take it up, if you wish."

---

(2)
The four machine guns in the wings had adhesive patches over their muzzles to keep the dirt out. When the guns were fired, the patches were blown off. The mechanics could see this when the aircraft returned to the circuit, and knew that there had been a scrap.

"That won't be necessary, thanks, Chiefy. By the way, I'm sorry I got a few holes that need patching."

Chiefy relaxed, smiling. "The lads are already at it," he said quietly.

I saw the Commanding Officer the next day, and told him the oil pressure story. I was, I suppose, a bit contemptuous, although I tried not to be. I couldn't understand Jack's behaviour. It was completely foreign to me. And I knew I couldn't fly with him again.

"You will understand it, in due course, when you are a little older," the C.O. responded gently. "Not everyone possesses your enthusiasm for tackling the enemy. There is such a thing as legitimate fear, with which we must show magnanimity. The alternative is to destroy this man. I agree with you that this island is not the place for Jack. But there is another job for him. Non-operational flying, I should think, where he will be useful. I'll look after it."

The Squadron Leader was a very reasonable man. He stood up behind his desk, and I knew the matter was closed.

I went back to dispersal; it was our turn on readiness.

A section of four Spitfires of 249 Squadron RAF over the Island of Malta.

Junkers Ju 88, an excellent aircraft. Crew of four included very resolute gunners.

Anti-aircraft guns in Malta durning a bombing raid.

German bombers hit Takali aerodrome in Malta.

Chapter II
Work and Play

Part 1

(Ref. Map: Malta, Sicily and Italy)

March 3rd dawned another beautiful spring morning with not a cloud in the sky. It would be a good day for flying, and the Huns were up in force. But it was not to be a good day for the boys on our side of the Malta Channel, that seventy miles of Mediterranean that separated us from Sicily.

It started at 0815 hours, when four Spitfires from 1435 Squadron took off from Halfar to sweep over southern Sicily. The pilots who had lots of enthusiasm but very little experience were trying to raise some Messerschmitts, and in this they were successful. Air Vice Marshal Park had previously sent a message to London requesting only experienced pilots. There was no time for learning in Malta, he had told them. But Fighter Command couldn't find enough fellows with experience, and had to ship out young nineteen-and twenty-year-olds who hadn't yet seen an aircraft with crosses on the wings.

The German listening post at Noto, near Sicily's southern tip, picked up the approaching Spitfires. The Luftwaffe controller scrambled six Me 109s in adequate time. South of Comiso, Sicily, the 109s made a classic attack on the four Spits from above and behind, and it was all over pretty quickly. Three Spitfires went down; one pilot was seen to crash into the sea, and two baled out. The fourth pilot managed to return alone to Malta to tell the tale. The only good news he had was that at least one of the two who had baled out was down in the sea very close to the Sicilian coast, and we might be able to pick him up.

From Malta, our air/sea rescue launch courageously put out to search the sea for survivors. The first escort for the launch was by four Spits from 229

Squadron, led by my chum Steve Randall. 229 Squadron shared Krendi dispersal with us; we were all one happy gang of generally irreverent and occasionally irresponsible pilots.

"Steve" was not, in fact, my friend's name at all, although it was months before we found out that Steve was actually Bruce, and by then it was too late. Anyway, it didn't matter. Most of us were called odd names, some of them rather rude.

Steve was the most altruistic fellow that I had ever met, and this day, for him, was no exception. His section of Spits was successful in finding the 1435 Squadron pilot just off the Sicilian coast, and stayed with him until they were able to direct the rescue launch to the dinghy. The rescued pilot turned out to be Pilot Officer Taggart. There was no sign of McDougall or Vine, and the launch took off smartly on the return voyage. In spite of circling around relatively low down only about ten miles from the Luftwaffe's main aerodrome of Comiso, Steve's section was not attacked by 109s.

At 1005 hours, I was Tiger Red Three of 249's section of four Spits airborne to relieve 229. Just as we were taking over from Steve's section, flying north at 7,000 feet, ten miles off the coast, I saw a twin-engined aircraft far below us, outlined clearly against the blue sea.

"Tiger Red One. Red Three here. Aircraft ten o'clock way down on the sea proceeding north. Looks like a Junkers 88. Over."
"Tiger Red Three. Red One here. I got it. Attacking now."

Pilot Officer Oliver went down on the German aircraft in a standard rear quarter attack at good speed, firing, then breaking down and away in order to present as little target as possible to the rear-firing gunner. Although we were near the Sicilian coast and the Junkers was only three minutes from land, there was no possibility of the Luftwaffe pilot escaping our height advantage. But as we had learned with Ju 88s, the rear gunner's fire was effective and dangerous.

"Tiger Red Section. Red One. Be careful fellows. Make it fast. The gunner is accurate."

Red Two, Sergeant Stark, went in after his leader and was met by a hail of fire coming up from the 88 before he got within range. Nevertheless, he bored in and fired at the Junkers before breaking down, away and up again. Up again to get some height to bale out.

"My engine's had it. Tiger Red Two baling out." Stark's message was short.

I was next in, and thought that an unconventional attack might be best against this difficult gunner. The Junkers was not right on the water, but about 800 feet above it. I dove down to sea level, dead behind the Junkers with a good deal of throttle, depending on my excessive speed to offset the disadvantage of breaking upwards after the attack. When I pulled up from sea level at exactly 400 mph with the Junkers overhead, I had a perfect view of its belly, and took a very short but clear shot at the starboard engine. It immediately exploded in fire. Then I was climbing vertically and pulled back to roll off the top. In spite of my speed, the Junkers' gunner punched a few holes in my tail, but no harm was done. Now the Junkers was going down, one crew member baling out, but too late, hitting the water with a partly opened parachute. I saw Red Four go in near the doomed aircraft, to be met by a hail of fire from the very determined rear gunner, still firing just seconds before he died.

Steve's section watched our scrap and continued to escort the motor launch until the Junkers went in, returning to Malta quite short of fuel. We continued the escort. The launch stopped to pick up Sgt. Stark, and then we all went home.

Half an hour later, a large gaggle of Me 109s circled at 20,000 feet, twenty miles north of Malta, no doubt in response to the activity and the loss of the Junkers 88 near Sicily. 185 Squadron was on readiness when the controller scrambled four Spitfires, followed by a second section a few minutes later. Banker Green Section, the first four Spits, was climbing at 17,000 feet when the Messerschmitts attacked out of the sun. Two old acquaintances, Jerry Billing and George Mercer, had the fight of their lives. At least they seemed like old acquaintances. Three months constituted an old friend in those days.

The problem was that the "twelve plus" Me 109s (which in controller's jargon meant twelve or more), were above Jerry Billing's four Spits, and were divided into several sections making it impossible to observe them all at once. On the first attack, in spite of Jerry's breaking up into the 109s to meet them head on, they seriously damaged his number two, George Mercer's aircraft. George got into a spiral dive and had great difficulty controlling the aircraft. However, he got back to base and made a reasonable landing on one wheel, his aircraft full of holes and with part of the engine cowling missing.

Green Three and Four had lost Green One in the mêlée following the first attack. This was not an uncommon occurrence; high speed aircraft got quickly separated. Unfortunately, it resulted in Jerry's being left alone with a half-dozen Me 109s.

On the next attack, Jerry broke hard to starboard, the Me 109 overshot, and Jerry got a good crack at him observing strikes on the wing root. But at that instant, all hell broke loose. Cannon shells exploded in Jerry's instrument panel and engine, tearing off the back of his left glove. His controls were gone, and glycol coolant drenched his face and body. He had opened his canopy and his straps were undone, but now he was in a vertical dive at over 400 mph, and couldn't get out of the Spit.

He told us later, "I finally got my knees up and my feet on the control column, gave a mighty kick forward, and I shot out of the Spit like a cork out of a champagne bottle."

Tumbling over and over, he pulled the rip cord, the 'chute opened with a rough jerk, and he looked down at the blue Mediterranean three miles below, just in time to see his aircraft hit the water. He had wrenched his neck because he hadn't had time to take off his helmet which was still connected to the aircraft's radio and oxygen.

But he was O.K., and he found himself suspended seemingly motionless in silence. Such beautiful silence after so much noise and clatter. "Maybe this is heaven," he thought. Then he saw Mount Etna at 11,000 feet away off to the left, and his sense of humour returned. "Well, I certainly did my damnedest to get to heaven today"

On his right, Malta was twenty miles away. Then he saw the white caps below and suddenly remembered he couldn't swim. He pulled the CO_2 release, and his Mae West inflated perfectly. He had just inherited a beautiful pair of flying boots from Sergeant Carmody who had been shot down the week before. Poor Carmody had worn his old boots that day. Reluctantly, Jerry took one of the black leather boots off and dropped it, to improve buoyancy. It disappeared in the distance far below.

(The boots were part of an innocuous custom that had evolved. When a pilot failed to return, it was usual for his closest friend to help himself to an item or two of his clothing. We thought it was fair. I had struggled back late once and force-landed at Takali aerodrome near the west end of Malta, then bummed a truck ride to Krendi, and found that my only pair of silk pyjamas, bought in Gibraltar, had been confiscated. I really didn't give a damn for them, but I knew Chappie had them, because he had bought one pair in Gib too, on the same spontaneous whim. I got mine back, and two weeks later I got Chapman's too.)

Just above the water, Jerry dropped his second boot and then jettisoned his parachute as he hit the water. He thought he was going down a long way but soon popped up on the surface and inflated his dinghy.

Meanwhile, the controller sent up a section from 229 Squadron to look for survivors. How Steve Randall found Jerry in the rough water, I do not know. Don Goodwin, another Canadian, was flying with Steve, and only with difficulty could they keep Jerry in sight. They could not see his dinghy in the whitecaps, so thought that it had not inflated. With perseverance, Steve undid his harness, his parachute, then the dinghy on which he was sitting, opened his canopy, and flying low and slowly, threw his dinghy to Jerry. This was the second time Steve had done this trick. The first, to a chum in the English Channel a year earlier, had been a lifesaver.

The motor launch, directed by Steve and Goodie, wasn't long in picking up Jerry.

The day's score in aircraft had gone badly against us. We had lost five Spitfires and had shot down only the Junkers 88. We had lost two pilots — one killed and one presumably a prisoner of war. But three pilots had been rescued from the sea. The Luftwaffe had lost more aircrew: a Junkers 88 normally carried four men.

That afternoon, the Wing Commander thought that we might yet be able to improve the day's score. It was 249's turn, and we were keen to go and have a look at their main fighter base. We circled around Comiso at 21,000 feet for half an hour, but the 109s were content to let well enough alone, and didn't rise to the bait.

Jerry Billing of Windsor, Ontario, was shot down three times, kept coming back, and got his share.

Steve Randall (right) of Toronto and the author, Krendi airstrip, Malta.

Part 2

(Ref. Map: North Africa)

The next day, March 4th, Steve Randall, Greg Cameron, "Frithy" and I got a week's leave in Tripoli. Jerry Billing and some other pilots from 185 also got a week off, but we didn't go together and we never caught up to them.

Tripoli had just been captured from Rommel's Afrikakorps by the British Eighth Army on January 23rd. The port was found severely damaged, the entrance blocked by sunken ships. But within ten days, supply ships were entering the harbour to support the Eighth Army's advance on Tunisia. It was only five weeks since the war had gone through, and the city didn't have much to offer us, but at least we got off the island for a week, our only leave while in Malta.

An Officers' Club had been set up in the Uadden Tripoli hotel, from which we watched an exciting bombing raid the first night. We cheered on the gunners, with shrapnel falling like hailstones, until the wardens chased us indoors. We loafed a day or so, but inevitably got restless and hitch-hiked a ride to Cairo in an American Dakota cargo aircraft. It was a terrible ride across twelve hundred miles of desert, the heat of the March sun already reflecting from the sand and bouncing the C47 mercilessly. We stopped only once en route, at Benghazi, for grateful refreshment. And we marvelled at the pyramids and the Sphinx as we approached Cairo. Were they 3,000 or 4,000 years old? We weren't sure. We poked around for a day and a half, staying pretty close together because of the unsavoury characters peddling knives on the street. We were not enraptured with Cairo, but enjoyed the change of food at Groppi's Restaurant.

Steve and I bought crepe-rubber soled shoes which looked good, but were full of cardboard and fell apart after three weeks. And Steve bought a ukulele. It was hanging up outside the door of a dingy shop. It was small, barely two feet long, with four cat-gut strings. Steve took it off the hook, tuned it for a couple of minutes, then started to play "Five foot two, eyes of blue. Has anybody seen my gal?"

"Three pounds," the vendor asked.

"Robbery," said Steve. And it was. We were all Flying Officers at the time (and likely to remain so indefinitely), making seven bucks a day.

"One quid", said Steve.

"Thirty shillings," the Arab countered.

Steve gave him the thirty bob and without further ado sat down on the store keeper's stool outside the door and began to play "I'm in love with you, honey." When I joined in, Steve switched to tenor harmony, for which he had a natural facility, and very quickly a smiling Arab audience began to gather. We were into our third song (we only had three) when a string broke on the ukulele.

"I'll get some cat-gut in the shop," I offered.

"If he doesn't have any," Cam joked, "there's lots back at that first restaurant we tried, the one with the four-legged chicken." Actually the chicken was probably goat.

Then it was time to go back to Tripoli, and we were rudely confronted with the fact that all those empty east-bound transports were now filled to capacity, going back up to the front.

We were in a night club. I don't recall the name, although it may have been Shepherd's. At any rate, it was full of servicemen from all three forces, with a lot of chatter, drinks, and smoke. Someone proposed that we might be pilots sent back from the front to pick up new Kittyhawk fighters for the squadrons up there.

It seemed like a champion idea, a very reasonable way to get across a little more than a thousand miles of desert. But we had never flown Kittyhawks, and had no helmets (therefore, no radio), no gloves, parachutes, maps, nor even a water bottle. But an aeroplane is an aeroplane. We could certainly fly them if we could get them started. We might just pull it off.

We decided to have a crack at it. We were only four days removed from Malta, where conditions were conducive to thinking more of the present than of the future.

The first thing that we had to do, since we would never be authorized to fly an aeroplane about which we knew nothing, was to learn how to start a Kittyhawk. They were American aircraft (or "planes" as they called them), with Allison engines, and had almost nothing in common with Spitfires. But if we could start them, we could certainly get airborne.

So in that night club mélange we found a pilot who had flown Kittyhawks, and he wrote out, on the back of a Player's cigarette packet, how to start the aircraft — and each one of us memorized it. It was vital to know how much to prime the engine, how to get the gear up and flaps down, et cetera, because we had to do it right on the first attempt. We learned that there were new Kittyhawks sitting on an aerodrome at Helwan, a short ride from Cairo.

Although we had no maps, I had drawn an approximation from a map on the hotel lobby wall, with a pencil and two sheets of paper, marking the wiggles of the North African coast. We would fly in a loose formation to El Adem near Tobruk, a little over four hundred miles, where we would have to stop and refuel.

The next morning we caught the train to Helwan, and one really does have to literally "catch" that train: run like hell, jump and hang on with hundreds of people inside, outside, and on top of the coaches. When the train slowed down near Helwan, we jumped off and walked in through the gates of the airport.

Inside the gates new Kittyhawks were lined up, with a few airmen poking around. We each chose one, and announced to the airmen that we were down from the front to pick up these new aircraft, and were they ready to go and full of fuel? On being assured that they were, we got in, using our little bit of luggage as a cushion. The parachute bags which we used for travelling were amusingly appropriate. Who were the poor airmen to question officers in uniform? Did they notice that we didn't have 'chutes or helmets? We couldn't use the radio. Was there a controller?

All of the knobs and levers in the cockpit were exactly where the fellow in the bar had said they were, and my aircraft started promptly.

I felt some relief when I looked around and saw the props on all four aircraft turning over nicely. We were airborne smartly. There was nothing unusual about flying a Kittyhawk, although it reportedly had a mean tendency to spiral in a dive. But it seemed terribly underpowered, as indeed it was, compared to our Spits in Malta.

We turned north-west toward El Alamein, then flew westerly across the recent battleground where the Eighth Army had finally forced Rommel to retreat. So many burnt out tanks, trucks, and guns left behind down in the desert! And so many young men too, I knew. Then the miles of criss-crossing tank tracks down in the sand made me think that perhaps this was the right place for two great armies to fight it out, rather than repeat the stalemate of France in the First War. But I knew that the battlefield would be extended up into Europe, and that the war still had a very long way to go. This did not depress me; on the contrary, I found the El Alamein battleground a stimulating sight, and was keener than ever to get back to Malta.

Two hours later we landed at El Adem near Tobruk, and refuelled our Kittyhawks by hand. Nobody said a word to us, and we bunked in a tent for the night.

"What do you think of this kite, Steve?" I asked. We always called our aircraft "kites".

"Wouldn't pull the hat off your head," Steve replied.

"It pulled yours off, Steve," Cam said, and we all laughed.

Steve had forgotten that he had a cap on, not a helmet, and when he opened the canopy before landing (which was routine in a fighter aircraft in case of dumping it over) his cap went sailing off into the desert.

"Thank God we have Spits in Malta. These are awful bloody aircraft," said Frith, the only Englishman in the foursome. He wasn't happy. He didn't like this trip one bit. This wild scheme was going to get us all into trouble. He had only reluctantly gone along with us.

"You're right there, Frithy," I agreed. "I tried full throttle climb. Only sixteen hundred feet a minute. Pity the poor blokes that meet a 109 with that performance."

And yet there were at least four squadrons doing exactly that. In one of them, 260 Squadron, Stocky Edwards from Battleford, Saskatchewan, was having great success against the Messerschmitts in spite of the definite superiority of the Me 109G (1475 H.P.) over the Kittyhawk III (1150 H.P.)

Next morning we got airborne again. There was so much sand blowing that Steve and I circled while waiting for Cam and Frithy. Frithy was O.K., but Cam appeared to be unable to get his landing gear up, and after flying a few miles with us, he wagged his wings and turned around and went back to El Adem. We three continued to Benghazi, refuelled, and went on to Marble Arch. The great white arch that Mussolini had erected could be seen for miles, beautiful but functionally useless. Somehow it seemed to exemplify Mussolini. I had no time for him at all, and figured that we would soon fix his hash one way or another.

We had come another 250 miles from Benghazi, and arrived in a sandstorm. There were no buildings at Marble Arch, only two rows of forty-five gallon drums, painted white, to mark out the landing strip in the sand. From the air I saw a tent part way down one side. I landed, taxied off the strip between the barrels, and parked the Kittyhawk near the tent. As I was closing the canopy to keep the sand out of the cockpit, Steve pulled up beside me.

The howling wind was blowing so hard that the sand burned my face. The tent was flapping noisily. Steve and I sat down on some ammunition cases. The lone occupant, an airman, was on the 'phone, shouting above the wind to be heard. He tipped his head to the left, and sand ran out of his ear. Then he took the phone away for a second, tipped his head to the right, and sand ran out of that ear. I'd never seen this trick before, and Steve and I broke out laughing.

We hadn't yet had a word with the bloke on the 'phone, when Frith came in through the tent flap. He sat down beside me and mumbled some words. Then he said it again, and I caught something about "Send my stuff down here from Malta." Steve hadn't heard him with the wind.

"Frithy, what the hell are you talking about?" I asked. Steve looked up. "When you fellows get back, send all my stuff down here," Frith repeated. "What's the matter, Frithy?" Steve asked. "Go outside and take a look," Frith replied dejectedly.

Steve and I went out into the sandstorm and we could just make out the fuselage of a Kittyhawk sitting on its belly near the tent. It appeared to have cartwheeled.

"Busted all to hell," would have been the Malta description. It was a write-off.

Frithy had apparently lost control in the sandstorm and had hit a few sand-filled barrels. We hadn't heard a thing with the wind. Now we knew what he was talking about. In Malta, aircraft were so valuable that if a pilot broke one, it meant a posting to the desert, the worst possible punishment. Frithy thought that he might as well stay right here, at Marble Arch. Save a lot of travelling.

We went back into the tent. We were laughing like two idiots at the idea of Frithy sitting in the tent with the bloke with the sand in his ears. It really was hilarious, and seemed to get funnier by the minute.

"What the hell is so amusing, you silly bastards?" scowled Frithy. "God damn Colonials. I told you this was a damn fool scheme."

Steve wiped his eyes. "Frithy, smarten up, for God's sake. We're laughin'." That was Steve's favourite expression. It wasn't literal, although we were laughing at the time. It meant "Everything's under control."

"Steve's right, Frithy," I said. "Nobody knows us. Nobody knows we have these bloody aircraft. We didn't sign for them. We're not Kittyhawk pilots. I never saw a Kittyhawk in my life, did you, Steve?"

"Never," said Steve. "Don't know a thing about them."

"Right. Frithy, this is what you do. Leave the bloody thing right where it is, and jump on the next aircraft that comes through."

Frithy was feeling a little better. "Do you think so, Steve?"

"Absolutely, Frithy," Steve replied knowingly. "Everyone knows that the spoils of war are left behind."

And that is precisely what Frith did. When the wind settled down a bit, Steve and I refuelled, and got airborne. Not long after, a Hudson came along with a few supplies for the airman on the phone. Frith got the last seat, and found Cameron already comfortably ensconced having a snooze. Cam had gone back to El Adem when his landing gear wouldn't retract. He said he almost got trapped into chasing one "whirling dervish" sand eddy after another, deep into the desert. They looked like aircraft taking off. Then he smartened up and flew back north to the coast and found Tobruk. He landed, and sometime later another Kittyhawk landed and pulled up beside him.

"This is my lucky day," thought Cam as he transferred his baggage to the other Kittyhawk, and took off. Cam was refuelling in Benghazi when the westbound Hudson stopped in. They had two vacant seats, so Cam got aboard.

Steve and I concluded that we probably should not fly right into Castel Benito airport at Tripoli, so after a two hour flight, we dropped the two Kittys off at Sertan, near Misurata, about a hundred miles short of Tripoli. There was a Repair and Salvage Unit there, 53 R.S.U. Steve and I jumped out of the Kittyhawks quickly, told an N.C.O. that we had just ferried these aircraft up from Helwan near Cairo (which was more or less true), and had to move smartly to catch a ride in a Baltimore that had landed just behind us.

We were welcomed aboard the Baltimore, destination Castel Benito. Steve nearly forgot his ukulele and had to run back to the Kittyhawk to retrieve it. Then it was just under an hour to Tripoli's airport, where there were dozens of service vehicles. We were offered a lift into town by an Army Officer in a Jeep.

"Where's your cap?" the Captain asked Steve, somewhat officiously. He was insinuating that Steve was improperly dressed, which, of course, was true.

"Tobruk," said Steve.

"Tobruk is an awfully long way from here," said the Captain, looking at Steve. "Over seven hundred miles, I would say."

"It's an awfully long story," offered Steve.

The Captain had trouble figuring out young Air Force officers, and let it go. He told us where to find a military clothing shop, and Steve got a new cap. It looked stiff as a board, but no doubt the guys in the mess would soon pour beer into it, and that would fix it.

Steve and I were buying some dates at a street vendor's stand when we saw Cam and Frithy coming toward us.

"How's it going guys?" asked Steve, nonchalant as ever.

"You and your damn schemes!" said Frith. "This is absolutely the first, last and only time that I'll ever go on leave with bloody Canadians! By God that's true!"

We sat down on a bench under a palm tree. Cam was chuckling when he told us about borrowing the other guy's Kittyhawk at El Adem. Cam had never seen a guy with sand running out of his ears. We could hardly eat our dates.

After a while Frithy was laughing too. Steve pulled the ukulele out of a paper bag and began to sing.

Chapter III
The Uncompromising Sea

No warning sound that morning in the sun,
Black crosses flashed blue wings that held the gun:
A fiery aircraft plunged into the sea;
It took my friend, and left a lesser me.

(Ref. Map: Malta, Sicily and Italy)

We didn't do as well as we would like to have done in the spring of 1943. Of course, we went on the offensive over Sicily, and generally speaking, offensive fighting will lose more aircraft and pilots than defensive, simply because the scraps take place over enemy territory and survivors are not picked up. And some of the fellows who baled out over the sea on the way home were lost, in spite of the competent rescue service.

There were some Messerschmitt pilots at Comiso, Sicily, who were masters of the hit and run tactic. It was legitimate. They would attack from high above, usually directly out of the sun, at high speed, one very quick pass only, then disappear, impossible to catch, leaving one or two of our boys going down in smoke. If the victim was lucky, he could bale out; if not, there wasn't a word.

So it was with Jack Dawkins. The yellow-nosed Me 109 flashed between us, and black crosses on pale blue wings disappeared far below. Perhaps one second had elapsed. Not a word from Jack, his aircraft leaving a long trail of smoke.

Newberry and Goodyear, Tony Notley and Don Cruse, Wing Commander Ellis,[1] Davidson and young Sheehan. Not a word. The loss of Squadron Leader MacLeod, our C.O., wasn't quite the same. He was boldly bombing a train very close to Comiso airport, and the 109s didn't let him get away with it. Likewise the C.O. of 229, Tommy Smart, attacked Comiso itself, right into the hornet's nest, and most likely picked up flak from the airport. He got half-way back to Malta before baling out. But he used the old roll-over technique and got caught, his boys said, and didn't get clear of the aircraft before it hit the sea.

Low-level bombing and strafing were high-risk jobs. There was always a great deal of flak coming up. Before you even pointed your nose at them, they started to let you have it. All the lights from the tracers looked like harmless fireworks and tended to mesmerize one. I never liked strafing as much as air combat, but some fellows like Steve and Goodie made careers out of setting transports on fire and blowing up trains. And arguably, theirs was the more important contribution. And they got away with it for quite a while.

On March 20th, Withy and Miller were strafing when Withy got hit by flak. He had to bale out half way home. Miller was circling Withy's dinghy when Me 109s jumped him and shot him down. The Walrus flying boat went out to pick them up, escorted by Browne and Locke of 249. These two fellows were also jumped by Me 109s, and killed.[2] It was our second bad day in March.

---

[1]
Eventually we learned that our quiet, respected Wing Cmdr. John Ellis was a prisoner of war.

[2]
*Christopher Shores, the British air war historian, with H. Ring (German) and W.N. Hess (American) wrote in 1975, in **Fighters Over Tunisia**: Saturday 20 March 1943, "Two claims were made by Luftwaffe pilots (flying Me 109's near Malta): Hpt. Sommer of II/JG 27 claimed one Spitfire at 16:32, probably Browne, and Hpt. Tonne of I/JG 53 claimed the other, probably Locke. Browne apparently was shot down by Sommer, a Danish volunteer in the Luftwaffe. Hpt Sommer was reportedly tried [for treason] and shot after the war in Denmark."*

In April and May, we were still dive bombing and strafing whatever we could find that warranted such action in Sicily, and we improved our score in the air in Messerschmitt 109s, Junkers 88s, and Junkers 52s. Flying Officer Cyril Gosling, a tall, quiet chap from North Battleford, Saskatchewan, got four or five 109s and Ju 88s very quickly before we lost him in the Sicilian invasion.

Sometimes we were lucky with aircrew who were down in the water. On April 15th, a Wellington from 40 Squadron in Malta was returning from a raid on St. Marie du Zit airfield in Tunisia when it was shot down by a night fighter. We were out with long-range tanks four days later, doing a square search about 120 miles south-west of Malta. We were just turning port ninety degrees, from north to west, when I noticed a slight wisp of cloud off to the east. It wasn't anything. We continued west. Then I changed my mind; better go back and take a look. I turned 180 degrees and went east for four or five miles, and there was the whole crew in a bomber dinghy. It was their last flare that had made a wisp of smoke. I dove down at the dinghy crew to celebrate, then pulled up to a couple of thousand feet to call Malta and get a vector for the Walrus flying boat. The boys were O.K.

At this time Goodie's luck ran out and he got shot down. Goodie was, properly speaking, Don Goodwin. But he detested anything proper. He had come from Maynooth in the central Ontario lumber country. He was a very competent pilot. But he hated spit and polish, orders, rules and regulations, and military discipline of any kind. He had no ambition to assume responsibility; he just wanted to fly. He went where the RCAF and RAF sent him, and never complained. He had a perpetual half-smile on his face, due, I believe, to his natural joie de vivre. He refused to take any aspect of life seriously, and lived entirely for the moment. It was a rare ability.

I had been on 421 Squadron with Goodie in England a year earlier, and when I caught up to him in Malta, he told me that he was sorry about my bike, but he was chuckling when he said it. He was always chuckling over something. We had been issued bicycles because it was about two miles from the mess around the airport to dispersal, and I had lost mine and got charged for it. Goodie had, of course, lost his, and had taken mine. "You see, Hap," he said, "there was this lovely girl and we were going across that field next to the airport, and the damn bike got in the way so I left it in the hayfield. I'm sorry about that."

Goodie's rebuttal of all rules and regulations contributed to his problems when he baled out about half-way between Malta and Sicily. His 'chute worked fine, but he had never bothered to learn the routine of inflating his Mae West or dinghy, and forgot to discard his parachute just as he entered the water. He got all tangled up in the shrouds under water, and later said, "That was when I died."

The sea was rough with white-caps; it would have been bad enough that day in a dinghy. But Goodie forgot to take his flying boots off, had the uninflated dinghy tied to his rear-end, his uninflated Mae West, and the hopeless tangle of the parachute. He fought hard and swallowed buckets of salt water for several minutes until his strength and air gave out. He last remembered fighting toward the surface which he could see but couldn't reach. He couldn't hold his breath any longer and had to take a gulp of sea water. He knew from experience that nobody would find him in the rough sea. He said to himself quite calmly, almost without emotion, "This is it, this is what it is like to die." He gave up struggling and lost consciousness. And that was why he later said to me: "That was when I died," and as an afterthought, "It really wasn't too bad." Typically, he did not complain.

Goodie was not located immediately. We could not find him in the white-caps from the air. But a launch crew thirty miles out from Malta was about to turn around when they bumped into something. Something brushed against the hull. It was Goodie, bobbing up and down, unconscious, barely alive, still tangled in his parachute. They hauled him aboard.

Some considerable time after Goodie's escape from the uncompromising sea, I learned of the loss of Squadron Leader Geoff Warnes in the English Channel. Geoff was a giant of a man with a heart as big as his frame. He was from Yorkshire, and probably twenty-five when he was our Flight Commander in 263 Squadron in the fall of 1941 in south-west England. Each of us young nineteen year olds, just recently operational, would have followed him anywhere. I was elated when he took me with him as his number two a few times across the Channel. It was my first thrilling look at France. We were flying low-level in Whirlwinds, a beautiful single-seat, twin-engine fighter. I remember that initially I was apprehensive that we would run into some Messerschmitts, but after fifteen minutes I was afraid that we wouldn't. But Geoff knew that I really wanted to fly Spits and wished me luck when, with some reluctance, I left 263, posted to a Spitfire squadron.

I was not surprised to hear that the affection which Geoff's pilots felt for him did not diminish. He was C.O. of the Squadron which had been re-equipped with Typhoons. Returning from France, his engine failed over the wide western end of the Channel. He baled out but was very difficult to see in the rough water, and appeared to be struggling to get into his dinghy. Flying Officer Robert Bruce Tuff was circling over Geoff, and called up to say that he was going to bale out and help the C.O. The rest of the Squadron tried to dissuade him, to no avail.

F/O Tuff was last seen very close to S/Ldr Warnes in the water, but with deteriorating weather and fuel shortage, their squadron had to leave them. They were never seen again. It is not known whether this very brave act by the young Australian pilot from Seddon, Victoria, has ever been recognized.

* * * *

It is only ninety miles across the narrow stretch of the Mediterranean between Marsala at Sicily's western tip and Cape Bon, Tunisia. All convoys to Malta from Gibraltar had to pass through this Sicilian Channel, and it was almost impossible for the slow-moving convoys to avoid detection, even if they had managed it up to that point. In April, 1943, with the Tunisian campaign going full tilt, these narrows were busier than they had ever been during the battles in the desert. Aircraft were constantly flying across from Castelvetrano to reinforce and supply the Luftwaffe and Afrikakorps. It was difficult not only for slow-moving convoys to get through. Even Royal Navy destroyers, proceeding toward Malta at good speed, while they would have welcomed a U-boat challenge, had difficulty running the gauntlet of air attacks.

Two Royal Navy destroyers making a run for it on the night of April 15th were attacked, probably by Heinkell 111 torpedo bombers, perhaps by Junkers 88s as well. This occurred near dawn on the sixteenth, some forty miles north of Pantellaria. One destroyer was hit and set on fire, being severely damaged below the water-line. The other stopped, and rescued the crew before the stricken vessel sank.

At 0645 hours, Tiger Red Section of four Spitfires from 249 Squadron was airborne from Malta. We had long-range belly tanks attached, and were told to go out and find a destroyer in the channel north of Pantellaria, and escort it toward Malta. We were not advised that there had been two destroyers, and that one unfortunately had been lost. This was not surprising because the action had just taken place. No doubt the Navy was busy sorting out signals and didn't have time to give the details to RAF pilots. Our job was simply to prevent any further attack on the remaining destroyer.

On this lovely spring morning with the sun on our tails, we flew north-westerly at deck level, our props turning over just above the water. After thirty-eight minutes, about 140 miles out from Malta, we sighted the destroyer dead ahead. And at the same moment, we saw a Junkers 88 close by the ship; we had arrived just in time.

The pilot of the Ju 88 saw the Spitfires and turned smartly toward Sicily which was visible about fifteen miles away. He was about one thousand feet above us, and had an excellent aircraft of approximately the same maximum speed as a Spitfire Five at sea-level. We were compelled to attack quickly from below to prevent his escape.

Three of us attacked. Pilot Officer Oliver saw his fire hitting home. I was second in, pulling up with full throttle, no time to gain speed, attacking from low starboard to port.

A few good bursts and the Junkers was on fire. That had not been difficult; my problem now was my lack of speed in getting out of there. I was a fair target and the rear gunner let me have it. My windscreen was suddenly completely covered with oil as I broke down and away from the Junkers toward the sea. I didn't go too low because I could see nothing except through the side. I pulled away, then up to 1500 feet, prepared to bale out if necessary. But my oil pressure needle never moved. Through the side perspex,[3] I saw the Junkers 88 pilot moving smartly to set the burning aircraft down on the water, his quick action the only hope for his crew.

Still my oil pressure and temperature remained constant! It appeared that I had sufficient oil to continue flying, and that I was not suffering any further loss. The oil tank is a concave metal tank in the nose of the Spit, just below the spinner. I thought that such a sudden loss of a considerable quantity of oil might be due to a hole in the upper part of the tank. If it were a ruptured oil line, I would have lost it all very quickly.

A Spitfire is small, and the cockpit is snug. I found that by slowing down, loosening the harness, opening the canopy, and carefully reaching around with my left glove tight to the curve of the perspex to prevent the slipstream from pulling my arm rearward, I was able to wipe the oil off the windscreen, and obtain moderately good vision ahead. No further oil appeared on the windscreen, so I seemed to be O.K. for the moment.

---

(3)
The perspex was the clear plastic sliding hood that covered the cockpit. Only the windscreen was made of two-inch bullet-proof glass.

I flew down around the destroyer, some of whose crew waved from the deck. They had seen the Junkers go down. But of greater consequence, although I was not aware of it at the time, they were relieved to be underway again toward Malta, to feel and hear the throb of the diesels from the engine room. Anyone who has ever been on board a small naval ship at sea will appreciate how anxious the crew become when the vessel stops in the water. They know they are sitting ducks for a torpedo. Jack Long, a Maritimer, and I learned about that anxiety when our convoy[4] was attacked by submarines on the way out to Gibraltar from Londonderry. Then a severe storm came up which frustrated the U-boats, but which Jack and I enjoyed, laughing at the water coming over the bow of the sloop. Jack loved the sea; his favourite song was "Harbour Lights." Ironically, he died shortly after we arrived in Malta when he was shot down into the sea.

After an hour, 229 squadron relieved us, right on schedule. We flew home at 2000 feet, in case I had to bale out. Some strato-cumulus clouds were beginning to form in the warming sun, and I nipped through a cloud and came out with a clean windscreen. But I didn't clean all the oil off the belly, and the mechanics spotted it in the circuit. The senior N.C.O. was there when I switched off.

There were two, nice, clean holes, entry and exit, through the oil tank about half-way down. I had lost half my oil, but the Merlin engine hadn't missed a beat.

More importantly, I knew that I had to smarten up on my attack. It was elementary tactics. One could slide in behind an enemy fighter at approximately his speed. But there were no exceptions to the rule that an aircraft with a rear gunner had to be attacked at high speed with a clean breakaway leaving a minimal target.

---

(4)
  This convoy was part of Operation "Torch", the Anglo-American landings at Oran and Algiers, Nov.8, 1942. Pilots were transported out to Gibraltar by whatever Royal Navy ships could accomodate us, thence we flew Spitfires to Algiers and Bône.

A few minutes after we had turned over the destroyer to 229 Squadron, another Junkers 88 appeared, much to the joy of 229. They promptly dispensed it into the sea, they informed us on their return to Krendi.[5]

Ken Goodyear, Steve Randall and Don Goodwin were all shot down; the latter two survived.

(5)

Shores et al also refer to the April 16, 1943 event in their book **Fighters Over Tunisia.** *"At 0645 four Spitfires from 249 Squadron left Malta to escort two destroyers to the island; these were found at 0730 15 miles from Sciacca, one burning, the other stationary in the water. At the same time a Junkers 88 of III/KG 76 flown by Oblt. Henrich Oldendorf, Staffelkapitan of 8 Staffel, was seen. All Spitfires attacked, F.O. Kennedy, P.O. Costello and P.O. Oliver hitting it; the starbound engine caught fire and the bomber ditched in the sea, but not before return fire had damaged Kennedy's fighter".*
"II/KG 76 reported the loss of a second Ju 88 to fighters near Pantellaria that day."
Note: As previously described, 249 Squadron pilots found only one destroyer afloat.

Cyril Gosling DFC from North Battleford, Saskatchewan,
229 Squadron, Malta. An excellent pilot.
(Killed over Sicily.)

Jack Long from St. John, N.B., loved the sea and "Harbour Lights". (Killed in Malta)

A Malta convoy is bombed. The ship barely visible on the left is firing at an aircraft. Malta got very short of food in 1942.

Chapter IV
A Very Good Ride

Squadron Leader John Lynch was our third Commanding Officer in 249 Squadron in the four months since I had arrived in Malta. His predecessors had been popular, and he had big boots to fill.

There was Timber Woods, tall and dark with a ready smile. We liked him, a good leader. He had flown a great deal of ops., was decorated, and was sent off for a rest a couple of months after I joined the squadron. Timber didn't enjoy the non-operational job, and came back as Wing Commander for his third tour as soon as his six month stand-down was over. By then we were up in Italy, and Timber and his good chum Bowie Debenham, Commanding Officer of 126 Squadron, who had returned to operations with him, attacked a large gaggle of Me 109s over Yugoslavia, having crossed the Adriatic from Grottaglie. We never heard from them again. But I'm ahead of my story.

Mac MacLeod took over from Timber. MacLeod was a pilot's C.O., and his fortitude was not confined to the air. We were, of course, short of aircraft due to enemy action. Understandably, accidents due to carelessness were not tolerated. The routine punishment for a pilot who pranged an aircraft was immediate banishment to a squadron in the desert, which was only a couple of hundred miles to the south.

One day, one of our fellows ran off the strip at Krendi, broke his landing gear and prop, and faced the wrath of the Wing Commander who happened to be at the dispersal. Quite a few of us tore over to see the prang. Before the Wingco could say a word, MacLeod stepped between him and the unfortunate young pilot and said quietly, "Sir, if you send this man to the desert, you'll have to send me too." We thought it was superb. The Wingco was on the spot, but maintained his composure. The young lad stayed with us.

Squadron Leader MacLeod, from Pictou, Nova Scotia, only signed my logbook twice (two months) before he was killed over Sicily, an unsung courageous airman.

John J. Lynch was an American. From one of the Carolinas, as I recall, although he didn't have a drawl. I had known him briefly at Operational Training Unit (OTU) up near Newcastle in the summer of 1941 when we were flying Hurricanes. Then we went our separate ways, he to an "Eagle" squadron while I flew Whirlwinds for nine months before wangling a transfer to Spits. Johnnie was several years older than most of us, and had flown privately before the war. He was a very sober, taciturn individual whom the mechanics promptly labelled "Smilin' Jack." But if one could break through his shyness, there was a smile underneath. It just wasn't easy to find.

Johnnie was a keen student of the tactics and habits of the Luftwaffe, and spent endless hours in the Intelligence Room, reading reports on German and Italian sorties over the Mediterranean. The research involved Junkers 88 action against shipping, and transport aircraft, mostly Junkers 52s, carrying cargo to and from Rommel's army in Africa.

Johnnie had already taken me over to Sicily the previous month. We each had two 250 pound bombs under our wings, and went on a low level raid up the railway line north-west from Gela until we found a train which we blew up. Shortly after dropping the eleven-second delay bombs, we pounced upon a Junkers 52 transport aircraft which we clobbered. As Flight Commander, he had the privilege of attacking first, and he set one engine on fire before I had a crack at it. I knew that he was generous to share it with me, although technically it was RAF policy that any pilot who observed strikes on an aircraft shared in the claim.

Based on his reading of radar and radio reports, Johnnie got permission from Operations to make a daring long-range low level sortie northerly up the east coast of Sicily, across the Straits of Messina, then down onto the sea again north of Sicily proceeding west towards Palermo. He thought two aircraft would be optimum. We would be more than two hundred miles from home, but by staying low and maintaining radio silence, surprise should be our greatest advantage. There would be a reasonable chance of finding some enemy transport aircraft, but such a flight could not be undertaken more than once. The Luftwaffe fighter squadrons in the south of Sicily would not allow it.

One day, he asked me if I would accompany him early the next morning. I was absolutely thrilled with the prospect, and found the evening long. We got the mechanics to put ninety-gallon long range fuel tanks on our aircraft, doubling our endurance to three hours. These external belly tanks could be jettisoned whenever we were through with them.

The morning of April 22nd dawned cloudy, but visibility was good and we were airborne early at 0610 hours. We flew at deck level north-east around Cape Passero, then turned north about ten miles off shore. Opposite Riposto, I saw an aircraft coming south at deck level between us and the coast. Should I break radio silence so early? This might foil our plans. On the other hand, it might be the only aircraft encountered. I called up the C.O.

"Tiger Green One. Green Two here. Aircraft eleven o'clock ahead, same level, proceeding south. Over."
After a pause, Johnnie came on. "Green Two, I don't see it."
"Green One. Aircraft is now at nine o'clock. Might be a Junkers 52." It was a few miles away.
Another pause and the C.O. came back. "I can't find it, Green Two."

We were going in opposite directions and whatever it was, it was now at seven o'clock and required drastic action. I pulled around hard to port and said, "Green One, I'm going back after him. I'll catch him before we lose him," and I opened up the throttle.

It was no time until I caught up with the transport aircraft which proved to be a Ju 52, oblivious to our presence. As Green One was still a long way back, I gave the Junkers a quick burst which set the port engine on fire. It crashed into the sea at once. Then I turned back north, the C.O. also turned, and we continued on our course without a word. I could not understand why he had taken so long to react, but felt justified in my attack.

As we approached the Straits of Messina at Taormina, we turned port and climbed north-west overland, descending to sea level again south of the Lipari Islands. We were now proceeding westerly in brilliant sunshine, the clouds all having been left on the east coast. I was staring at three very small specks a long way ahead of us that at first I considered might be birds, but because of their constancy of position must be aircraft. I watched them for another minute or so, then decided to break radio silence once more.

"Tiger Green One. Green Two here. There are three small aircraft, possibly 109s, twelve o'clock deck level. I don't know if they're approaching or going away. They're several miles away. Over."
"Green Two, keep your eye on them. I don't see them yet. Over."
"Roger, Green One."

We kept on the same course and speed for perhaps three minutes more, although it seemed longer, by which time it was obvious that the three aircraft were going away from us, and that we were only very slowly gaining on them.

"Green One. Green Two here. Those three aircraft are still dead ahead and going the other way. We'll have to open up. Over."
"O.K. Green Two. Lead me to them."

Now that was better! We'd give the old Spitfire Vs a ride. Enough of this loafing! I opened up to nine pounds of boost. We still had lots of gas: still running on our drop tanks in fact. Now we were catching up a bit, and with that came a surprise. They were not 109s. I could see an engine in each wing. They had been so far away that they had looked like small aircraft, but now I saw that they were heavier.

"Green One. The three aircraft dead ahead are twin-engined. I'm opening up a little more. We must catch up more quickly. Over."

"O.K. Green Two," came the reply from the C.O., but still he lagged a thousand yards behind me, making no move to lead the way.

I weaved a little to starboard to look back at Johnnie, then straightened out again looking at the three aircraft still a long distance away, and felt in the middle of a conundrum. I knew that the C.O. was full of courage; he had carefully planned this flight. I knew also that he was a very conservative pilot and didn't like to abuse his aircraft. But this was going on too long since we had originally broken silence; and yet he was the boss. I opened up a bit more.

I was intent upon the silhouette of the transport aircraft ahead when I finally realized what was happening. It must be the C.O.'s eyes. He couldn't see the enemy aircraft yet. He had said, "Lead me to them." He was myopic as blazes and hadn't told anyone because he knew that he would be grounded at once. It would be the end of operational flying for him. In a way, he was using my eyes. I felt relieved, and keen to get this job over.

I caught up to the three transports flying in open formation about two hundred feet above the water. Now I could see that they had a third engine on the nose like Junkers 52s. I moved in on the port quarter of the nearest aircraft at good speed, but for a second I noticed the mid-upper gunner's gun pointing to the sky. Then I saw his head on his chest; he was snoozing. There was no time to think about the gunner, and anyway I wasn't interested in him. My target was the port engine which I hit a good clout, and which promptly caught fire. As I pulled out I thought, "I reckon that woke him up!" The aircraft descended quickly to the sea. Did he crash or ditch? If the latter, the pilot did very well, but I was busy looking at the others.

The C.O. was still out of range, but coming in quickly now. I had a belt at the second aircraft, another port engine with profuse black smoke, while Johnnie attacked the third which went down on fire. Then I hesitated. I held off while Johnnie hit the second aircraft another clout before it settled down on the water. I distinctly remember feeling that I should be a little diplomatic here. Besides, I was content. Elated! I was not angry with the transport crews.

There was nothing difficult about these clumsy aircraft. But they were enemy aircraft, and I had clobbered some port engines, and they were down in the water.

"Green Two, Green One here. Let's go home."
"Roger Green One."

We climbed hard to the south. Johnnie had taken over once more. We had been hidden behind the mountains of Sicily, particularly Mount Etna at 11,000 feet which had cut us off from any radio contact with Malta. With our noses high in the climb, out of habit I looked in my rear-view mirror. In the broad view of the sea a thousand feet back I could see three fires burning on the water. Small, localized fires, quite apart from each other, and I thought, "They were not carrying fuel."

We climbed up to 22,000 feet and Green One called Malta Control. Control came back loud and clear, which was reassuring because we were still one hundred and sixty miles away. Control appeared excited.

"Tiger Green One. Where have you been? We've been trying to get you for an hour. The whole German Air Force is up after you. Over."
"Hello Control. Tiger Green One here. We've been to a party. We're coming home now. Over." I could tell Johnnie was chuckling.
"Tiger Green One. Control here. Keep your eyes open. Several squadrons of 109s are up from Comiso looking for you. Did you have any luck? Over."
"Hello Control. Tiger Green One. We got four Junkers 52s. Over."
Then he continued to me: "Green Two, did you hear Control?"
"Roger Green One." I felt fine. I thought that Control was exaggerating. I was enjoying this.

The C.O.'s eyesight was terribly defective in scanning the horizon for an aircraft, but he could see the outline of Sicily from 22,000 feet and knew exactly where we were. Of course, Etna's volcano was just to our left, coming up half-way to meet us. The southern tip of Sicily was seventy miles ahead, and Johnnie wasn't through with the Huns yet.

"Green Two. These guys have a problem lookin' for us. We'll just go down and take a look at Comiso and show them where we're at." Johnnie's southern background had finally surfaced.

We stuck our noses down and opened the throttles. I stayed with him about a hundred feet abreast. We were moving, because the controls were a bit stiff, but it was not a time to look at airspeed. I was busy looking for the 109s and finally, looking straight ahead as we tore across Comiso aerodrome at nought feet. I looked right into the hanger at men scattering in all directions. We were rubbing it in.

Tiger Green One throttled back when we got down over the sea. In no time the Malta cliffs rose up ahead of us, and we pulled up over Krendi.

He waited for me, and we walked in together from the aircraft. He was much more affable than usual, smiling, in fact. I was chuckling over the Comiso bit.

"That was a good ride, sir," I said. "A very good ride."
"Yes, it was, actually," he replied. "Actually" was his favourite word. He had picked it up in England, and unconsciously used it a lot. "What are you going to claim?" he asked me.

I recalled his sharing one with me before. And perhaps he would take me again.
"What about sharing even, two each? I asked.
"Sounds reasonable," he said. He seemed relieved.

We went into Intelligence. I never mentioned the matter of his eyesight. It seemed of less significance on the ground. Besides, it was none of my business. I knew that Johnnie, like other Americans who had joined the RAF before Pearl Harbour, was considering transfer to the U.S. Army Air Force. He had served the RAF very well; to fly with him was my privilege.

Wing Commander Timber Woods (right) and Squadron Leader Bowie Debenham moved the Malta Wing to Italy, where they boldly attacked thirty 109s but were lost.

Johnnie Lynch, DFC, American, C.O. of 249 Squadron. Spring of 1943, Malta.

Chapter V
"Scramble Red Section"

It was a beautiful June day without a cloud to mottle the contrast of the light blue sky above the dark blue Mediterranean. From our landing strip close to the edge of the rock, we could see where the sky and the sea met away off to the east. It looked like an infinite distance, as, of course, it was.

Everything in Malta is close to the sea. The island is only twenty miles long and six miles wide. It's a small place to find if you're coming in from the north-west in bad weather and the island's radio is on the fritz. Fortunately, that doesn't happen often. Sitting there in my aircraft, waiting, I smiled at the memory of a scramble in pouring rain, ten-tenths low cloud, and half a dozen different vectors to 10,000 feet before Control went off the air. Loss of radio contact was not a problem in fine weather, but when visibility was poor we were very dependent upon the island's radar and the controller giving us a course home. On that rainy day we let down through cloud in tight formation, broke clear at 500 feet, and found the island before fuel got low. Perhaps I should have phoned Control after we landed, but I didn't wish to add to their embarrassment.

Some tiny fishing vessels bobbed like corks on the calm sea a few miles away, and my musing continued. While elsewhere momentous decisions on the conduct of the World War were being made by worried men who would be late for dinner, these local fishermen pushed away from shore with a pair of oars, and went out in their tiny boats, the way it always had been.

On the other side of the strip, a short, grizzled man kept two burros moving in a circle, tramping and threshing the grain with their feet on the hard-baked ground. This custom derived from the biblical fertile crescent at the far end of this blue sea, and hadn't changed in more than two thousand years. Perhaps both the sun-browned fisherman and the farmer with his tiny fields and neat stone fences knew that eventually, sooner or later, we noisy disruptive foreigners would stop fighting each other, pick up the trappings of war, and go home. Patience would be rewarded with a return to sanity.

We were on "Immediate Readiness," strapped into our Spitfires, sitting near the end of the strip. All was ready; oxygen and radio connected to my helmet that hung on the reflector sight. A mechanic relaxed beside a battery cart that he had plugged into the engine of the aircraft to guarantee a fast start, and conserve the aircraft's battery. When the phone call came from Ops Control to our dispersal, there remained only pulling on one's helmet and gloves, and starting the engine. We were expected to be airborne in less than one minute.

I had been loaned to 185 Squadron for a week or two. They were a bit short of pilots and anxiously awaited some new arrivals from England. I didn't mind too much with whom I flew, as long as I got airborne reasonably often. Didn't really mind, I reflected, but I had been with 249 Squadron for six months, and we were used to each other's habits. Mind you, there were always a few new green pilots who didn't know how to scan a bit of sky and know absolutely that there were no aircraft there. One hoped they would learn before they got clobbered. Or before they allowed a Hun to clobber the Spit next to them, whose tail they were supposed to be guarding. Anyway, I knew Billing and Mercer here at 185, and they were experienced and competent. But I didn't have them today.

The real compensation, however, was that I was strapped into a brand new Spitfire IX. The Malta squadrons were being re-equipped with "Nines" after a couple of years, including the blitz year of 1942, during which the Spit V was the defence of the island. Recently the Luftwaffe had moved their latest Messerschmitt Me 109G into Sicily along with some Focke-Wulf 190 squadrons. These latter were superb aircraft and the old Spit V just couldn't keep up to them. The Spit IX, a heavier brute in the engine but the same airframe with the lovely loose ailerons, an additional 250 h.p., a four-bladed prop, and a a supercharger that came in with a tremendous kick at 21,000 feet, once more gave us the advantage of a superior performance. We were full of enthusiasm.

"Readiness" was a state that one got used to pretty quickly in Fighter Command. Whether in England or Malta, or supporting the army in the field, a fighter squadron had to take its turn on readiness to defend against a Luftwaffe attack. It meant long days, pre-dawn till dusk. Those on the pre-dawn duty were roused at 0330 hours in the Malta summer, and after a breakfast of toast and coffee, powdered eggs and stewed tomatoes, trundled off in the back of a Bedford van to the landing strip dispersal. After placing one's helmet and gloves and 'chute in the aircraft, and a chat with the mechanic who ran up the Spit in the dark, the waiting game in the dispersal began. It ended either with a "Scramble" call from Ops., or relief from duty by the other flight at 1300 hours.

Normal three minute readiness allowed us to lounge in the dispersal, wearing our Mae Wests. With bad weather, Ops. might put us on thirty minutes and let us go to the mess. But when action was imminent, we were moved up to an "Immediate" state and strapped in. And that's the way it was today.

At 1440 hours, a red flare went up from the dispersal hut, arching over the strip, and my mechanic jumped to his battery. I pulled on my helmet, fastened the oxygen mask, put on my gloves, turned the oxygen valve on, and primed twice. The engine broke into a roar. The mechanic pulled out the battery cable and gave me a "thumbs up" and I was tearing down the strip with full throttle and 3000 R.P.M. Airborne, gear up, throttle back a little to let the lads catch up, at 4500 f.p.m. climb.

"Malta Control. Bullet Red Section Airborne," I radioed as Red Two and Three formed on either side of me. We normally flew as a section of four, but we were strapped for pilots these days.

"Bullet Red One. Control here, Vector three six zero max climb to angels three zero. Three bandits possibly Me 109s approaching from the north at twenty-eight thousand. Over."

"O.K. Control. Bullet Red Section max climb north angels 30. Over."

Air Vice Marshal Park, Air Officer Commanding (AOC) Malta and the boss of Control at Luqa, knew this game very well. He had been in charge of Eleven Group, that area of south-east England most actively engaged in the Battle of Britain, two and three quarter years earlier. He taught his controllers well, and now one of them was getting us north of the Huns so that we might be in a position to intercept them from 30,000 feet. Control was tracking at least three Me 109s proceeding south over us to the island. Probably there was one photo-reconnaissance Me, and two Me 109G escorts to protect him. Photographs of the shipping in Valletta harbour were taken almost daily, the information interpreted and relayed to U-boat commanders. Allied convoys to Malta suffered terrible casualty rates. Sometimes more ships were sunk than got through from Gibraltar to Malta with food, fuel and ammunition.

"Bullet Red One. Control here. Confirm position."
Our superchargers had just kicked in. We were moving.
"Hello Control. Bullet Red Section at angels two four, about one five miles north. Over."
"Bullet Red. Turn one eight zero degrees port. Continue climb to angels three one. You should see three bandits dead ahead over Grand Harbour. Look out for a few pointer rounds ack-ack shortly. Over."

"O.K. Control. Bullet Red turning south." We continued to climb and just over two minutes later I saw the Messerschmitts. Three black bursts of heavy anti-aircraft fire from the island helped me find the tiny aircraft glinting silver in the brilliant sunshine.

"Tally ho," I called. "Bullet Red Section. Bandits dead ahead. A little below." We were at 31,000 feet. They were perhaps four miles away and already losing height in a wide sweeping turn to starboard over Grand

Harbour. Now they straightened out on a northerly course with their noses down, and I knew they would be exceeding 400 mph. They would be across the seventy miles to Sicily in ten minutes. Unless we could do something about it, that is.

I had the throttle open and I rolled over and headed on a course to cut the angle toward the 109s, which had separated a little. I wound on nose-heavy trim so essential to keep the aircraft in a high-speed dive. The Spit responded eagerly as I dove more steeply than the 109s, with Red Two and Three no doubt following, although I could not see them. The controls got very heavy as the airspeed needle moved far right at 480 mph. (Corrected for altitude, true airspeed approached 600 mph.)[1] I could see that I was gaining on the nearest Me 109. That was something new. We were already half-way to Sicily; that was no problem. We knew from years of experience, dating back to the boys who had been in the Battle of Britain, that the 109 with its slim thirty-two foot wing was initially faster in a dive than we were. But we accepted that compromise happily in exchange for our broad superior-lift wing with its better climb and turn. One couldn't have it both ways. In any case, I was closing on this Me 109, which I recognized as a G. Perhaps he wasn't using full throttle.

We were down to 5,000 feet and our dive had become quite shallow. I could see the Sicilian coast a few miles ahead. Now I was within range at 300 yards, and I let him have a good squirt. The first strikes were on the port radiator from which white smoke poured, indicating a glycol coolant leak. I knew I had him before the engine broke out in heavy black smoke.

And at that moment, a good burst of tracer fire went over my starboard wing, quite close to the fuselage. I had lost the third Me 109, presuming it was away ahead.

---

[1]
Appendix 3

"Must be behind me!" I thought, as I skidded hard to port, then broke around. But there was no 109, only two Spitfires coming toward me. I thought the nearest inexperienced pilot mistook me for the 109. It happened not infrequently. But he was a bit out of range, and he missed, and I forgot about it at once in the same way that one forgets about flak that sails harmlessly by the wingtip. Much later I thought that I should have chastened whichever one of the two fellows fired at me, but at the time I felt that the guilty party knew that he had made a mistake, and I let it go. I think that many of the fellows developed the same somewhat nonchalant attitude toward getting shot at.

We landed at 1525 hours, having been airborne only forty-five minutes. I stopped to have a word with the mechanics who were looking after EN533, the serial number of this aircraft from the factory in England. The Squadron letters hadn't been painted on her yet.

"This is a beauty, lads," I said, making finger marks on the blue smoke stain that extended back from the six stubby exhaust stacks, a stain that clearly showed a hard climb six miles up. "A superb aircraft."

The Intelligence Officer came out to the aircraft to meet me, a very unusual move for that reticent fellow. He waited for me to jump down off the wing.

"You got a 109," the I.O said, smiling broadly.

"I believe so," I answered. "It caught fire after I got him in the port radiator. But how did you know?"

"Ops called up. Thought we'd like to know. They picked up the pilot's panic call to Comiso for a flying boat. Engine on fire. He was baling out about ten miles south of Pozzallo. He's in the drink."

"Well, that's good," I said, when he finally stopped. "That's where he belongs. In the bloody drink!" I admitted feeling some satisfaction from the confirmation of the Me 109G, because it was an excellent German aircraft.

But we had to refuel and rearm, and get back quickly on readiness.

About half an hour later, I was back on immediate readiness, strapped into my aircraft, when the Intelligence Officer climbed up onto the wing of the Spit.

"We have a little problem," he said. "I know you shot down that 109, but your number two claims that he fired at it too. Do you mind sharing it with him?"

I was taken aback. I knew darned well that it was I at whom he had fired and very nearly hit. The 109 was 300 yards in front of me, and my number two was at least 500 yards behind me, because when I pulled around I found the two Spits. That meant that he was half a mile from the 109. But I rationalized that he had shared the danger, and it might help the young lad in the long run. I was reluctant to tell the I.O. that this fellow had, in fact, been shooting at me. And it was too hot, strapped in the cockpit, for a prolonged discussion. So I said "O.K.", and the I.O. jumped down off the wing.

If I had known these fellows better, and had I not been on loan to another squadron, I might not have been so easy. In any case, it was many years later that I learned in a letter from Chris Shores, that the I.O. had actually divided up the Me 109 among the three of us.[2]

* * * *

(2)

C.F. Shores, London air war historian, reported in private correspondence, 25 February, 1992: "10 June, 1943. The Bf 109 shot down over Malta by yourself, Red Two and Red Three, was a reconnaissance aircraft of 2(H)/14, flown by Leutnant Friedrich Zander. It was a 109G-4, ' Black 14.'"
(While we knew these aircraft as Me 109s during the war, and the Luftwaffe pilots also called them Me 109s after the designer Willy Messerschmitt, the historian points out that the correct designation is Bf 109 after the factory Bayerischer Flugzeugwerke. I hope that I might be excused for having used, in this book, the old name by which we knew them so well.)

Exactly one hour and thirty-five minutes after landing, Bullet Red Section was scrambled again to intercept "six plus" enemy aircraft proceeding south from Scalambri, Sicily. The controller vectored us north to Pozzallo at 16,000 feet.

We couldn't find any sign of the reported six aircraft, but a few miles south of Pozzallo, where we had been a little earlier in the afternoon, the long white wake of a flying boat's takeoff caught my eye before I saw the Dornier itself lifting off the water. It was obviously an air/sea rescue of the Messerschmitt pilot. The Luftwaffe was being very efficient.

"Bullet Red Section. Red One here. There's a Dornier flying boat just airborne below us. We're going down to have a look." Then I called Malta Control.

"Hello Control. Bullet Red One here. Dornier 18 flying boat just airborne ten miles south of Pozzallo. Presume he picked up the Me 109 pilot. What will we do with this flying boat? May we have a crack at it? Over."

The reply came back at once.

"Bullet Red One. Control here. Negative. Do not attack the Dornier. Repeat. Do not attack Dornier. Is this clear? Over."

"Hello Control. Bullet Red One. Message received and understood. We will leave Dornier alone."

By then we had dropped down to 3,000 feet, and I spied an aircraft that looked like a fighter tearing off straight north toward the coast. It appeared to have been escorting the Dornier.

"Some escort!" I thought. I called up the boys, who of course had heard my conversation with Control.

"Bullet Red Section. Red One here. We can't touch the Dornier but there's some bastard trying to get away about two miles north. Let's get him."

The sudden presence of the other aircraft which was fair game sort of salved our wounded pride. I felt like little Jack Horner who "put in his thumb and pulled out a plum." Rewarded for good behaviour, I smiled. I suppose we would have circled the Dornier and let the 109 pilot see who had clobbered him, although he wouldn't have known it, nor would he have known whether he was about to be shot down twice in one day. I know they saw us high-tail it after the Macchi 202, as it turned out to be.

Red Three, Flight Sergeant Sinclair, was closest to the Macchi and attacked first and got some strikes. I had a good crack at it from 200 yards. It began to smoke.

Sinclair called up: "The Macchi's on fire, Red One."

It was going down. We were still a few miles off the coast at 1,000 feet.

We turned around to head south to Malta. I passed quite close to the Dornier flying boat going in the opposite direction. I knew that there was a custom of chivalry about air/sea rescue operations. That was why I had called Ops. I also knew that the invasion of Sicily was imminent, and that some of our boys might be down in the water in the next couple of weeks. But I had mixed emotions as I looked through the perspex for a fleeting second at the pilot of the Dornier.

"You go to hell!" I murmured. I didn't know whether or not he had another passenger to pick up, and I didn't much care.

A section of 249 Squadron pilots on readiness in Malta.
McBain, Kennedy, Gervais, Keating.

Chapter VI
Adventures in Sicily

It was late afternoon July 9th, 1943. We were escorting a Liberator bomber squadron attacking Gela aerodrome in southern Sicily. At 24,000 feet we turned port into the sun. In an easy sweeping turn in tight formation, the twelve Libs dropped their noses to gain speed before dropping their bombs in unison. I was always fascinated by their technique of discharging the bombs from their bellies while in a descending turn at great speed. In spite of the centrifugal force, they were invariably accurate, and this time they laid their eggs right on the aerodrome. We crossed over from starboard to port above them, looking for enemy fighters. There were none. The 109s had evacuated Gela a day or two earlier.

As we turned south toward Malta, we could see the distant approach of three thousand ships and landing craft, steaming north. We had seen the armada approaching from the south, close to Malta, as soon as we had become airborne to join up with the Liberators. But now they were north of the island and joined by more vessels from Malta. Small, fast Navy destroyers and corvettes were tearing around the periphery of this great convoy like sheep-dogs keeping their flocks in order.

It was a thrilling sight, tempered by the thought that if any enemy aircraft were airborne, surely the crew would immediately radio that the invasion of Sicily was in progress! There was no turning back now. It was still daylight, and sixty miles to go. Could they possibly maintain the element of surprise? The strong winds and rough seas would give a false sense of security to the enemy. This was the greatest amphibious operation so far in history, and we had front row seats.

The North African campaign had been successfully concluded in Tunisia in May. In spite of Hitler's determination to hold Tunis against the combined British and American Armies' encirclement, 250,000 Axis troops, of which exactly half were German, surrendered. The myth of Nazi invincibility was destroyed. Rommel escaped by air, and von Arnim surrendered. When von Arnim was brought through Algiers on his way to captivity, it was suggested to General Eisenhower that he consider the custom of bygone days when a captured commander was the honoured guest of his captor. Eisenhower declined: he felt so strongly about the morality of the Allied cause that no compromise was possible. He did not wish to see any Axis general. Such was the mettle of our Commander-in-Chief of the Sicilian campaign that was about to begin.

For seven days we had been escorting squadrons of American daylight bombers; Fortresses, Liberators, and Mitchells which came north to Malta from African bases, picked up the Spitfire escort en route, and proceeded to Sicilian targets. We had slip tanks to increase our range. The timing was crucial in picking up the bomber squadrons and climbing up above them to afford protection. This pre-invasion bombing of strategic targets extended from Pachino at the southern tip, north to Catania, and westerly to Gela and Licata, including the airfields at Comiso and Gerbini. The American bombing chased the Luftwaffe out of southern Sicily, and by the time the convoys were approaching, our air superiority was firmly established. The seaborne landings began in the early darkness of July tenth. American, British, and Canadian forces began the campaign by capturing the ports and airfields by which their presence could be maintained.

We usually flew twice a day (our endurance increased to two hours with the small drop tanks), initially covering the beaches, then as the days went by, supporting the armies advancing northwards. We had control of the air, but there was less Luftwaffe activity than expected. A few days after the landing, some Spitfire squadrons of 324 Mobile Wing were operating from Sicily and, with the campaign going well, Malta was quickly becoming too distant from the front for a fighter base. Before long, most Spits would abandon the island for Sicily. Strategic bombers for the Italian campaign would take over Malta.

This was the way it was in the latter half of July, 1943, when quite a number of us fellows, ordinary pilots in the Malta squadrons, were "stood down." Stand-down was an RAF term commonly used when an aircrew member was taken off operational flying, and sent on a rest. All of us who had been on Malta for seven or eight months were posted back to Blighty.

"It's non-operational flying for you, for six months," they said. The island was emptying itself of all my old friends, the best and closest friends I was ever to have. Some of the boys were gone already; they had arrived a month or so ahead of me, when I got caught up in the North African landing.

All my old friends leaving, did I say? Not true. A dozen fellows with whom I had arrived would never be leaving. Luck had abandoned them.

On July twenty-first, my days with 249 Squadron ended. Squadron Leader Lynch signed my logbook and wished me luck. It must have been he, as Commanding Officer, who had recommended me for the Distinguished Flying Cross a couple of months earlier, but he never mentioned it. And I was as reticent as he when we shook hands. I hoped that he was not going to fly any more ops, but didn't say so.

Somehow, I was not content. I didn't feel the need of a rest at all. I just wasn't keen on the idea of going back to England to instruct. I had learned a great deal in Malta about air combat, and I felt in top form. And more than anything else, I was full of enthusiasm for the Italian campaign. And the way to get involved in that campaign was by joining 324 Mobile Fighter Wing. I knew that the five squadrons in that wing were to provide close tactical support to the British and American armies through Sicily and up into Italy.

So when they told me I was through, I borrowed my old aircraft and flew over to Comiso aerodrome, in Sicily. Comiso, which I had seen so often from 25,000 feet, the home of the Me 109s! Now some Spits were sitting there, and I had come to see the C.O. of 324 Fighter Wing, Group Captain Gilroy. I spoke to the adjutant first, and told him that I had been stood down in Malta, and would like to see the C.O., if that were possible.

I had heard of Group Captain Gilroy, of course. All of us had. He was a no-nonsense, greatly admired Scot who ran his wing efficiently. He was affectionately know as "Sheep" Gilroy by his peers. We thought it was because he had been a sheep farmer in Scotland before the war, and probably that was true. What there was no doubt about was that he was credited with seventeen enemy aircraft destroyed in the Battle of Britain.

"What can I do for you?" he asked, standing bare-headed in the sun outside his tent. He was accustomed to a lot of problems, and had lots to do, in spite of which he was politely seeing me without hesitation. I didn't want much of his time.

"I've completed a tour in Malta, sir," I answered, "and now I've been posted back to the U.K. I was wondering if you had any use for a good pilot?"

I surprised myself a little with my audacity, but that was the way the words came out. He may have been a little surprised too, or perhaps "relieved" would be more accurate. This was unusual. Young pilots generally went where they were sent without question.

He broke into a smile. "Well, young lad, I like your spirit!" He was used to making quick decisions. "Yes, we can use you. You may join 72 or Treble-One, whichever you like. Give your particulars to the adjutant, and we'll get in touch with Malta."

"Thank you, sir." I saluted and left with the adjutant.

Both 72 and 111 were excellent squadrons. I was thrilled. It didn't matter which, really. But I knew that George Hill was C.O. of 111. He was a very tough little guy from Nova Scotia, afraid of nothing. I had known him in England in 421 Squadron.

"I'd like to go to Treble-One, if I may," I told the adjutant.

"Looks like the Group Captain is going to fix you up," the adjutant replied. "Sit tight until you hear from us."

I walked back to my aircraft, pushed my cap down beside my seat, pulled on my helmet and gloves, and flew back to Malta.

It was only a few days later that I was flying with 111 Squadron out of Pachino. I was very happy to be flying what was officially called tactical support to the army in the field. We had a job to do. Living in a tent would be just fine. This was the place to be right now.

It was, after all, the soldiers, not we Air Force types, who were going to force the German army out of Sicily, defeat Italy, and maintain the momentum of change in the fortunes of war. There was no mystery. The maps in Intelligence supported the daily newspapers. Hitler had reached his zenith in 1942, but since November of that year, eight months ago, had suffered three major defeats at El Alamein, Stalingrad, and Tunisia. Now he was about to suffer a fourth, and lose his ally, Italy. And we were full of enthusiasm to be part of it.

Moving to Sicily from Malta did not change our flying duties significantly. We still escorted American bomber squadrons coming up from African bases, but now their attacks were less on airports, and more on tenacious defensive German pockets that were holding up the Allied advance on the narrow roads around Mount Etna. We didn't need the drop tanks any longer. The bulldozers made landing strips for us through the orchards and vineyards. Lemons and oranges, olives, figs and walnuts were pushed aside.

We lay in the shade under the wings of the Spitfires, eating luscious handfuls of blue grapes off the vine, ready to jump as soon as we saw the bomber formation approaching from the south. While they made one circle overhead, we would tear off in a cloud of dust, and catch up to them, climb above them, and head north. We flew about 1,000 feet above them and off to one side, to protect them from Me 109s.

But we could not help them with the flak that inevitably came up from the ground. We could only watch and feel grateful that we were free to move around while they were most vulnerable on the approach to the target when they held steady in tight formation in a gentle turn, never wavering. Then the heavy flak started pasting them mercilessly, black bursts of fragmented steel breaking in among the Fortresses or Libs, or twin-engined Mitchells, Marauders, and Bostons. Sometimes an engine or tail was completely severed from an aircraft. More frequently, an engine would catch fire, then the wing was ablaze, and one would involuntarily count the parachutes baling out of the crippled aircraft that had veered crazily off course from its mates.

"Come on, fellows. Get out of that thing! There should be seven parachutes!"

We escorted the wounded bombers to the southern tip of Sicily, then let them go, and went back to our strip in the vineyards.

The days were warm and sunny, the nights were clear. It seemed as though it didn't rain at all that summer in Sicily. I shared a tent with an unusual fellow, a quiet, gentle Canadian from Yellowknife, Northwest Territories. Jake Woolgar was a tall, lean, angular man with a deep bass drawl. His weathered face looked like that of a cowboy, but in fact he had been a bush pilot and prospector before the war. He felt that he should interrupt his prospecting for gold, and joined the RCAF. It happened that he had read about 111 Squadron, RAF which dated from the first war, and that had fascinated him. He could in no way account for the amazing coincidence by which he ended up in 111 Squadron in Sicily.

Jake had camped out for many summers, and he saw no point in pitching our tent in the warm Sicilian summer. So we folded our tent on the ground, lay on it, and looked at the stars, night after night.

Occasionally we went into a village that we had overrun, or more accurately, a village that the army had taken with hard fighting while we leap-frogged over it. The soft stone buildings were scarred. This was a new experience; we were not accustomed to being an army of occupation, and didn't use the term. We knew that this was only a temporary arrangement, and we had no wish to stay. We were obliged to wear our Smith and Wesson .38 revolvers, but luckily had no need of them. The Sicilians were genuinely friendly, gave us wine and sold us large, brown fresh eggs. We hadn't seen fresh eggs since leaving Canada, and on our first opportunity, bought a dozen each. The kind lady cooked them for us at once in a heavy iron frying pan. Four of us each ate a dozen eggs, absolutely the best eggs I have ever tasted.

In a war, very strong friendships are made in a very short time. I think it is probably because often a great deal happens in the course of a few days or a week. The only constant is change. So it was that this tall, lean prospector from Yellowknife and I developed a strong friendship. Eventually, Jake met a charming eastern European woman in Cairo, and married her. They went back to Yellowknife after the war. He asked me to join him. He knew where there was gold, and he found it. But I had other things to do, and that, as Robert Frost poignantly wrote, was "the road not taken."

There wasn't any doubt that the German troops had become rather unpopular in Sicily. Sicilians and southern Italians by nature are not warlike people. They held the view that the Germans had brought the war to their country, had eaten up what was edible, requisitioned the rest, and were going to cause the English to come next. But when the English came, the war would soon be over. They were generally not impressed by Mussolini's pursuit of grandeur and his alliance with Hitler. They dreamed of their sunny island all quiet again, and for the moment tolerated us with friendly smiles.

In an unconventional way, U.S. General Omar Bradley had quite a bit to do with the friendly attitude shown to us by Sicilians. A week after the Allied landing in Sicily, the U.S. 7th Army had 22,000 prisoners of whom one quarter were Sicilians, with plans to ship them back to the States. But Bradley noticed that all the crops in the fields were ripening with no manpower to harvest them. All able-bodied Sicilians had been conscripted by Mussolini. Bradley perceived that these prisoners were reluctant soldiers, and thought that it made economic sense for both sides to free them to work on the farms. He passed the word that deserters would not be picked up as prisoners. U.S. Army H.Q. disapproved, but it was too late. The clergy spread the word, Sicilians deserted the army and came out of the hills, and soon 33,000 were paroled to their homes and farms. Fascist slogans were removed from the walls in towns, posters of Mussolini defaced, and we bartered among friendly smiles.

One day late in the campaign, I thought it would be interesting to take the Jeep northwards up to the front to see what the army was doing. I found myself entering a small town, the identity of which I am not sure. The main street was completely vacant. Not a soul could be seen, and I was puzzled as to where everyone had gone. I stopped, and a moment later a Jeep with an Eighth Army Lieutenant, accompanied by a Sergeant, pulled up beside me.

"What in hell is the Air Force doing here?" the Lieutenant asked me. "And how did you get by us?"

"I just drove up the road from the south," I answered. "Wanted to see what you fellows are doing."

"You're in sniper danger here. This town has not been mopped up yet. There are German soldiers at the other end of this street," he warned, pointing down the road. His tone softened a bit. "I suggest you turn around and get out of here smartly."

I was saved further embarrassment by one of the most thrilling experiences of my life. Around the bend, the sound of bagpipes broke the silence, and as I turned the Jeep around, the pipes, as is their nature, quickly grew louder. The piper and a company or two of marching soldiers came into view. I believe that they belonged to the 51st Highland Division, which had come all the way across North Africa from El Alamein.

Suddenly the town came to life again. All the upstairs windows seemed to be thrown open while buxom women leaned out inquisitively, and children appeared in the doorways. Old men hobbled out of the alleys to see what this unfamiliar sound heralded; without doubt the German troops at the far end of the street heard, and knew exactly. In spite of the Lieutenant's admonition, I got out of the Jeep, came to attention beside it, and saluted the passing Highlanders. I have rarely felt so moved. It made my trip entirely worthwhile.

About the middle of August, our C.O., George Hill, was "stood down." The little tiger was going on a rest. And George was a tiger; there was nothing refined about his tactics when the enemy was sighted. George knew that the shortest and fastest route between two points was a straight line at full throttle, and that was the way he attacked every Hun. He came from Pictou, Nova Scotia, and had boxed at university before the war. He thrived on fighting.

I recall one evening in the mess tent just before he left. We had had a scrap with some Focke-Wulfs, and George had got one. With his usual gusto, he had nearly rammed it. He was sitting with a scotch in hand, and a grin on his pug face.

"You're the second best pilot in the RCAF," he said to me.

"That's very kind of you, George," I replied. "But it's not true."

"Yes, it is," he argued. "You tear into the Huns full throttle. You don't wait to count their bloody 109s and 190s."

"Well, I might be the second boldest," I replied, laughing, "but I'm sure that there are lots of better pilots."

"Nonsense! Audacity and tenacity are what I'm talking about. They're nine-tenths of the fight. Fancy flying isn't worth a damn!" George loved an argument and he wasn't about to lose this one, although I wasn't disputing his tactics, with which I basically agreed.

"And who's at the top, George?" I asked.

"I am the best, of course," he answered, laughing, and finished his scotch. While this was said in jest, George was so cocky and confident that he, to some degree, believed that he was the best. And he liked my flying because it was quite a bit like his own, although I preferred the quarter attack to his dead astern.

George and our Wing Commander had had a difference of opinion a month earlier. The Wingco insisted on disciplined flying, having learned the necessity of staying together in the great air battles over England, while George felt that with a lesser number of Messerschmitts available out here, every one should be clobbered immediately. Although my inclinations were similar to George's, the Wingco, of course, was right.

In any case, their difference was resolved a day later when they were returning, rather low on fuel, from Sicily to Malta. George saw a pilot in a dinghy, and circled him to give a vector to Malta for the rescue. But six 109s turned up and George had to quickly call up the Wingco, Cocky Dundas, for some help. In spite of being short of fuel, Cocky went back to George's aid, and dove through the six 109s firing, and pulled up to repeat the bravado tactic. The 109s took off for nearby Sicily. When the Spits landed, George thanked the Wingco, and they were friends.[1]

On August 17th, only thirty-eight days after our armies had entered the southern tip, the Sicilian campaign was over. Burnt-out relics of war were everywhere, including more than a thousand damaged or destroyed German and Italian aircraft that were left behind on the Sicilian airfields. The break couldn't have been more opportune for our squadron.

The idyllic weather was accompanied by a serious health hazard: a large number of us came down with malaria. It was impossible to avoid the malarial mosquitoes. We quickly learned that the only way to control the disease was by faithfully taking the prescribed daily quinine. The high fever, sweats, and weakness passed, and most of us were back flying again when we moved to Cassala, near Catania, on September 2nd. The next morning, September 3rd,

---

(1)
   Ironically, the pilot picked up by the rescue launch turned out to be an angry and rude German, When Cocky heard about it, he said that he understood his anger, but with his rudeness, the Hun should have been thrown back in the water.

at 0430 hours, our army crossed the Straits of Messina into mainland Italy, and we were once more airborne at 10,000 feet, covering the landings at Reggio.

Squadron Leader Peter Matthews, an Englishman who had flown in France in 1940 before that country collapsed under Hitler's onslaught, had taken over 111 Squadron from George Hill. He was much more conservative than the Nova Scotian, and there is little doubt that their different natures were to some degree responsible for their eventual destinies. Peter was still flying during the last year of the war, while George angrily (but never languishing) stared through the barbed wire of Stalag Luft 1 prison camp. On his second tour of ops., in April 1944, George had come too close to a Focke-Wulf 190, over France. He shot it down, but some debris came back and critically damaged his Spitfire. George force-landed, and was captured.

Another sunny afternoon, September 4th. We were up on our second trip of the day, a mélange of Spitfire Vs and IXs, with Squadron Leader Matthews leading us northwards up the Straits. Two Royal Navy destroyers far below and a couple of miles ahead of us, were moving out of the narrows of Messina. The ships attracted three Focke-Wulf 190s which had approached from the north and now were rolling over into a vertical dive toward the destroyers. The FW 190 was a superb new fighter of the Luftwaffe which had forced the RAF to re-equip its squadrons with the Spitfire IX. In this case, they had slung a 500-pound bomb under the FW 190. We considered bombing an abuse of fighter aircraft, but when the bomb was dropped, the excellent fighter was liberated.

I was leading the section on the starboard side closest to the Focke-Wulfs. I knew that with those superior aircraft, it was very quick action or nothing. As soon as I saw the Focke-Wulfs, I shoved the throttle of my old Spit Five wide open, stuck the nose down, and called up the C.O.

"Banker Red One. Yellow One here. I'd like to pursue three enemy aircraft that are bombing destroyers ahead. Over." I don't recall the C.O.'s exact answer, but he didn't say "no."

I watched the FW 190s dive, saw three bombs burst in the water very close to the ships, but harmlessly, I thought, and then the aircraft scooted away, high-tailing it northwards at sea level.

I thought that the FW 190s would probably turn easterly around Cape Vaticano; if so, we might catch them. So I cut across over the Cape and came down to sea level on the north side of Italy's toe, just in time to find the three FW 190s crossing in front of me. They did not see me as I moved in toward the nearest aircraft on the right. Now I was in formation with them, sliding in behind the nearest FW 190. I could not understand how they didn't see me, except that they must have thought that they were home free, and relaxed. The three aircraft, flying abreast, did not make a move. I let the one on the right have a good blast, and got a major strike, a large bright flash, behind the cockpit. This would have destroyed a Messerschmitt 109. But the FW 190, which was well armour-plated, and air cooled with no vulnerable radiator, took off with black smoke indicating full throttle, his companions doing likewise. My poor miserable Spit V was left behind, full throttle being about 30 mph too slow at sea level.

"Banker Yellow One. Red One here. What's going on? Over."
"Banker Leader. Yellow One here. Have wounded a Focke-Wulf and now pursuing. Over."
"Banker Yellow One, Red One here. You will not catch him. Suggest you rejoin squadron. Over."

The Squadron Leader was right. The three Focke-Wulfs were a mile away, and getting smaller. But Intelligence reports said that Luftwaffe pilots had been urged not to abuse their aircraft, to throttle back as soon as they could safely do so. Perhaps if I left the old Spit open for a few more miles they would slow down. It was worth a try.

"Banker Red One. Yellow One here. I'm gaining on the 190 now. Couple of minutes more. Over." It wasn't true, and I knew it.

Three or four minutes later, the C.O. was on again.

"Banker Yellow One. Red One here. Return to squadron. Over."

I had no answer for that. There was nothing to say, so I didn't try. The old Spit sounded fine, was well trimmed and wide open to get maximum speed, and was indicating exactly 300 mph at sea level. It would have gone much faster up in thinner air, but so would the Folke-Wulfs. I was a bit annoyed at these bloody Huns, probably because since first opening full throttle, twelve minutes had elapsed. I would have to watch my petrol now, because we were going further away from home. Somehow, it never crossed my mind that the three FW 190s might turn on me. They were running away. I had forgotten about my number two, Jackie Church, a New Zealander, and didn't want to turn to see if he were behind me, because that would lose further ground. I could have called him up, but I didn't think of that in the heat of the chase.

Just as we approached the coast of Italy's Gulf of St. Euphemia, the Focke-Wulf that I had damaged seemed to throttle back. It slowed down, and I caught up to him right at the beach. I hit him a good clout, and he went straight in, in a burst of fire.[2] I pulled the throttle away back and turned sharply, 180 degrees. Yellow Two, Flight Sergeant Church, was right behind me, and had been all the time. I was surprised that he had been able to stay with me, but pleased by his tenacity.

(2)
Christopher Shores, in private correspondence dated 23 March, 1992 reports:
"4 Sept. 1943. A Jabo (fighter-bomber) Focke-Wulf 190 of III/SKG 10 was lost on this date, reported shot down by a Spitfire near Cape Vaticano. The pilot was killed. There was no other claim for a FW 190 on this date than that of 111 Squadron." Mr Shores also confirmed that earlier that same day, Group Captain Gilroy had led 111 and 243 Squadron pilots over the Reggio landings, where they ran into a lovely mess of Macchis and Reggiannes. Seven were claimed destroyed for the loss of one Spitfire. But I was on the afternoon shift, and missed that party!

"That's the end of that bloke," Jack said to me, moving abreast so as to cover each other on our return.

"So much for the damned master race, Jack," I replied.

It had been a very long chase. Seventy miles. I did not like enemy aircraft, nor the guys that flew them. They were there to be shot down, and I had determined that not all of these 190s should escape.

Years later, I recalled the circumstances exactly, how I had felt and what I had said. One's mind doesn't lightly dismiss such emotional episodes, and I think it is best to tell the truth and not gloss it over. So I wondered whether my feeling and action had been fair, or justified, or neither. The immediate answer was the old one that had been said long before my time: "It was war, and all is fair in love and war." But I knew that that was a terribly inadequate answer, a platitude with the insinuation that love and war were exempt from the rules of fair play. There was, in fact, nothing fair about war. War, especially modern war involving civilians, is the antithesis of fairness. In war, fair play is not just irrelevant, it is counter-productive. We did not warn the Luftwaffe that we were about to attack.

What we were opposed to was this Nazi philosophy that their racial superiority justified the war against lesser peoples. We pilots who had already been in Britain and the Middle East for two or three years had not read Mein Kampf, but we were very much aware of Hitler's proclamations. In an earlier century Hitler might have been another Caesar, but in our generation there was an egalitarian restlessness afoot that doomed, probably forever, this repugnant thinking.

And so when the Focke-Wulf hit the ground in a great ball of fire, my first emotion was satisfaction at having overcome a Luftwaffe aircraft and pilot, – they went together. Whether the pilot baled out, or was killed, was immaterial; I felt no remorse. Air combat was an impersonal duel. No doubt some Luftwaffe pilots did not pay much attention to Nazi politics, but we did not and could not consider that possibility; the pilot of an aircraft marked with black crosses should be promptly shot down.

The impersonal aspect of combat did not preclude emotion. On the contrary, a hard fight was a most emotional experience, often including anger, and I have sometimes contemplated and understood how men, fighting against an invader of their homeland, have stood resolutely, and fought, and died.

I never thought of the pilot's identity. Only many years later, more or less accidentally, did I learn this fellow's name . . . But that is between us.

"Banker Yellow One. Red One here. Where in blazes are you?" The C.O. had picked up Jack and me talking. He was high over the Straits of Messina.

"Banker Red One. Yellow One here. We are on our way back, approaching the north end of the Straits. Over." In fact, we were still thirty miles from the Straits, on economical cruise, at 2,000 feet. In case either kite packed it in, we'd be able to bale out.

"Banker Yellow One. We're going home. Proceed direct to base. Red One out."

Jack and I picked up some anti-aircraft fire when we cut across the corner again at Cape Vaticano, but we didn't get hit. Obviously the Eighth Army hadn't got up there yet from Reggio. Well, it was only one day; they couldn't advance forty miles.

We got back to Cassala and landed with a few ounces of petrol to spare.

"You bastard," Jack said to me as we were walking in. But he was laughing. "We were a mile away from the 190 when you told the C.O. we were gaining on him."

"Thanks for staying with me, Jack." There wasn't much else to say. He had done what he was supposed to do.

When we told the C.O. that we had caught the Focke Wulf, he didn't admonish me. I knew that he wasn't entirely pleased with my behaviour. He had been justifiably concerned about the possible loss of two pilots and two aircraft to superior aircraft. He wouldn't have worried if we had Spit Nines.

And that, in fact, was exactly how this sortie ended. My old Five went to Maintenance, destination Training Command. It had had a good last ride. I got a new Nine, and it was a beauty. Now if I could just keep it a little while.

Jake, Rance, Johnny and Nobby of 111 Squadron, Sicily.
Jake Woolgar returned to Yellowknife after the war.

*George Hill, DFC and two bars, from Pictou, Nova Scotia,
a very determined fighter. DND PL 21682.*

*Mitchell B 25 medium bombers which we frequently escorted.
Note mid-upper gun turret. N.A.M. photo.*

Chapter VII
Foe or Friend?

It was said, in that summer of 1943, that the Italians did not possess a natural hostility toward the English and Americans, and that this accounted for their lack of enthusiasm in fighting the Allied invasion of Sicily. Certainly the Italians had fought well on the Allied side in the First World War, and their friendship with England and U.S.A. had continued between the wars. The large emigration of Italians to the U.S.A. during the inter-war period inevitably, in Italy in 1943, provoked the question among relatives, "Why are we fighting Americans?"

Surely Mussolini's delusions of grandeur, his dreams of being another Julius Caesar, were the cause of Italy's ultimate demise. Years earlier, Mussolini had got away with his bravado. It had been quite a while since he had been a local hero, but not so long that we had forgotten. As we camped in the lemon groves on the north coast of Sicily, somewhat impatient for what was surely our next move on Italy, we wondered what form that action would take.

I recalled 1936 when, as a fourteen year old lad, I used to read the evening newspaper aloud to my grandfather, whose eyesight was failing.

"Is Mussolini still bombing Haile Selassie's defenceless Ethiopians? Why is the League of Nations letting him get away with it?" the old fellow would ask.

And Mussolini's egocentricity continued. In June, 1940, when France was capitulating to Hitler and it appeared that the latter would inevitably invade England, Mussolini joined forces with Hitler and sent a few bombers against the RAF. The RAF promptly shot them down, and our Group Captain and Wing Commander had both been in that battle. It was therefore with nothing but contempt that we looked across at the toe of Italy, while we cleaned the oil and dirt off the bellies of our Spitfires in order to get another ten or fifteen mph maximum speed.

But we were not alone in our distaste for Mussolini. The loss of a total of 350,000 prisoners in North Africa, followed by our landing in Sicily on July 10th, persuaded Italy's patricians that they should change not only their leader, but their alliance in the war! On July 25th, Mussolini was arrested, and Marshal Badoglio, the senior general, became Prime Minister. The Germans, fearing that Badoglio would double-cross them, ensured that their own army got all possible equipment out of Sicily across the Straits of Messina in the few nights prior to the Allied entry into Messina August 17th.

"They wouldn't try it in daylight," was all we could say futilely.

On September 3rd (although we weren't told about it until September 8th), Italy surrendered unconditionally and signed an armistice with General Eisenhower, our Commander-in-Chief. As these events occurred, I noted the dates in my log book. These momentous developments in our relationship with Italy seemed, to us fellows in 324 Spitfire Wing, to be coming fast and furious. But we were doing what we wanted to do, and didn't give a hoot what the next move was as long as we could get airborne a couple of times a day. We were, however, intrigued when advised that the Italians were now on our side and had to be treated accordingly. Most of the Italian Navy had already sailed for our old familiar Grand Harbour in Malta. God, this was peculiar! Was Italy's behaviour also considered bizarre by our leaders? More likely, Italy's anticipated collapse was their chief justification for invading Sicily and Italy.

In any case, the Allied landing at Salerno Beach just south of Naples, took place on September 9th. We were airborne early, covering the amphibious landing forces, patrolling the beach at 14,000 feet. As it was two hundred miles north of our Sicilian airstrip, we required ninety-gallon, long-range drop tanks to enable us to stay over the beach-head for forty minutes. We flew two of these long trips on the 9th, and had a good view of General Mark Clark's assault. It initially went very well before General Kesselring took advantage of the high ground that ringed the beachhead. We saw a Junkers 88 over the beach, but he stuck his nose down and took off. We chased him for a few miles but he had too much of a head start. Besides, protecting the beach-head was our job. Reluctantly, we turned back.

Next morning, another fair day, we were airborne again, this time with Group Captain Gilroy of Battle of Britain fame leading 111 Squadron. The "Groupie" liked to keep his hand in, and flew with one of the squadrons in the wing whenever he could, but especially if there were a possibility of running into some Huns. He had a reputation, in his early days with the City of Edinburgh squadron, of spotting Me 109s before anyone else saw them. This was the first time that I had flown with him since joining his wing on August 1st, and I was ready to go.

On takeoff from Falcone strip, however, my Spitfire IX misbehaved and lost power; I very nearly flew into the lemon trees at the end of the strip. I had full throttle and full RPM but was only just airborne with absolutely inadequate power to clear the trees. For some reason I pulled back on the pitch control from 3,000 to 2,650 RPM, and the full manifold pressure instantly returned to this beautiful aircraft, and it leaped over the trees at the last second. God, how it jumped, rudely pushing me back in the seat. It was a new aircraft, and it was a beauty, although admittedly something was amiss at full RPM. But full power most definitely was there at 2,650 RPM, and I promptly forgot all about the lemon trees and joined Banker Blue One, G/C Gilroy, and the rest of 111 Squadron.

We arrived at Salerno Beach where the amphibious operation had begun the previous day. I thought it impossible to make any order out of the shambles on the beach of men and equipment, tanks and landing craft, smoke and flashes of guns and shell bursts. I was happy to be at 7,000 feet, unconcerned with the trajectory of the shells from the off shore ships that were bursting a few miles inland from the beach. At that moment, I saw and counted eight Focke-Wulf 190s dive bombing vertically at the south end of the beach, just north of Agropoli.

Blue One saw them too, because without hesitation he called, "Banker Squadron, Blue One here. Switch to main tanks. Jettison belly tanks. Attacking enemy aircraft now." We tore into the mess of Focke-Wulfs with alacrity.

I got involved with three of the FW 190 fighters which were staying right with me and turning with me as we descended to tree-top level. Fortunately, Hughie Eccleston, an Australian, picked off one of the 190s. It went in, in a great ball of fire. The second 190 disappeared to the south, but I couldn't shake the third at all, and couldn't figure it out. I should not have a problem out-turning a FW 190. I was pulling back as tightly as I dared, the aircraft was shuddering in a stall just above the trees, and I was swearing.

"What the hell's going on here?" I knew I was in trouble.

Was this Hun that good? Was he a better pilot than I was? A touch of doubt, just for a minute as I was almost brushing the trees. The trees! Stupid! I remembered the lemon trees with the loss of power on take-off. I yanked back on the pitch control, my boost shot up to 20 lb/square inch, and once more the aircraft leaped ahead like a thoroughbred. The Focke-Wulf pilot, unaware of how close he had been to victory, had wearied of the tree-tops and had taken off to the south with his mates, wide open throttle, the whole lot of them pursued by our squadron. I do not know how much manifold pressure I had been getting at 3,000 RPM because there was no time to look inside the cockpit in the midst of a scrap. But as on takeoff, it was hardly enough to keep me airborne. Anyway, it was irrelevant now that I had full power again.

It was not uncommon after a scrap that a chase might follow for twenty or thirty miles, if a fellow could lock onto the tail of a FW 190 or an Me 109. But the Luftwaffe fighters were almost always going the wrong way for us; that is, they were taking us away from our base. This chase was different and beautiful; we were all going south, and since we were on the way to Sicily, we were all going home. We weren't going home together, mind you, but it was a unique situation. And there was no fuel shortage. Now that I had solved this little boost idiosyncrasy, the true mettle of my steed became apparent.

I trimmed the aircraft to fly hands off, and started working my way through the pack of Spitfires from the back. It was like a horse race. I wasn't a lot faster than the others; I think we were all flying Spit Nines by this date. But in any case I went by one after another, just weaving gently through the pack, barely above the trees, until I caught up to the leading Spitfire.

This turned out to be the Group Captain, who, as was the custom, had his own initials on his aircraft. Out in front of G/C Gilroy, well out of range at about 800 yards, was the last Focke-Wulf 190, smoking a little black at full throttle.

I pulled up abreast of our Group Commander, just off his starboard wingtip. He looked over to his right at me, his face covered with his oxygen mask and mike.

"Do I stay here, or do I dare pass him?" I wondered.

I pulled back just a touch on the throttle for a couple of minutes. We were not gaining an inch on the Focke-Wulf. It was a delightful situation because I knew that the Group Captain was primarily interested in the Wing. But it demanded tact. He was the Officer Commanding, but surely he wanted someone to get that Hun up ahead! So I tapped the throttle forward the last half-inch, moved ahead (I must admit to a faint smile behind my oxygen mask), caught up to the Focke-Wulf pretty smartly, and hit him a good clout with everything I had, that is with both cannons and machine guns.

The German was a smart pilot. He pulled back on the stick at once, and shot straight up to 1,500 feet, baled out very quickly, and was coming down in his parachute when the Group Captain went by him.

"Who shot down that aircraft?" No call sign, but there was no mistaking the Group Captain's voice. Only five words, somewhat sharply, I still recall. "Blue Three here, sir," I answered, not quite sure of what was coming. "Bloody good show! Let's go home, chaps."

I need not have worried. The Group Captain turned to starboard over Lauria (we had chased the Focke-Wulfs forty miles), and led us across the Italian coast. We ran into some light flak from some of Kesselring's boys, who were being chased northwards by Montgomery's boys, until we got over the water and pointed toward Sicily.

After we had landed and hidden our aircraft among the lemon trees at Falcone, we gathered as usual at dispersal with the Intelligence Officer. Group Captain Gilroy came over to me.

"You're Blue Three, I presume," he said. He was straight-faced, but his eyes were crinkly.

"That's right, sir," I replied.

"Would you like to trade aircraft?" he asked. He was smiling now, and didn't expect an answer. He was pulling my leg, and I knew it, and I didn't give him one. He turned to talk to the I.O. He was a great leader, and only interested in the welfare of the wing.

Later, I told the mechanics about the boost discrepancy at full RPM, and that I had nearly flown into the trees. I also told them that it was the fastest aircraft on the squadron. "Don't foul up the manifold pressure when you fix it," I pleaded. "It's a beautiful aircraft."

"How much boost do you get?" asked the Flight Sergeant.

"Nineteen and a half pounds," I answered.

"Supposed to be set at eighteen," he explained, "but I don't think that has anything to do with the problem. We'll see."

I took JU-O (our squadron letters were JU, and this particular aircraft was O) back to Salerno Beach the next day. It behaved beautifully, and continued to do so, although I didn't have cause to push it hard during the next few days. Two of our fellows, Mellors and Plum destroyed two Dornier 217s bombing the beach-head, but I didn't see anything exciting.

Not so on the ground. Our initial successes were reversed when General Kesselring's Panzers counter-attacked very forcefully, and recaptured Battipaglia from the British on September 12th, three days after the initial beach assault. And on the following day, they re-took Altavilla and Perano from the Americans. We were getting ready to move up to a strip on the beach-head, but had to delay our plans when, for a couple of days, there was a very real danger that the beach-head would be lost. We flew a lot, and at least kept the Luftwaffe from significantly interfering with supplies to the troops through our control of the air. But it was the Naval shelling that really helped turn the Panzers back.

On September 16th, some of Montomery's Eighth Army coming up from Calabria in the south, joined forces with the Americans at the south end of Salerno Beach. The crisis was over, and we figured that we would be moving to Italy shortly.

Meanwhile, 93 Squadron, one of five in the wing, had suffered a large number of casualties in one way or another. They were away down in strength, and reportedly, in morale. Not only had the Luftwaffe knocked a few of them down, but some very rookie gunners associated with the amphibious operation, having sailed straight from the United States to Salerno Beach, did not recognize Spitfires overhead, and killed one or two pilots. A consequence of this was that nine months later at the Normandy invasion, all allied aircraft were painted with broad black and white stripes on wings and fuselage to eliminate such faux pas. Getting fired upon by one's friends was common in war, and was usually quickly dismissed. It only hurt when there were casualties.

We didn't get any black and white identification strips, but on the same day that the beach-head was relieved, Group Captain Gilroy re-built 93 Squadron with a new Commanding officer, Squadron Leader Westenra (New Zealander) two new Flight Commanders, Richardson (British) and myself (Canadian), and a half dozen new replacement pilots. I wasn't particularly keen on leaving a strong squadron like 111, my old friend Jake, and my new Spit IX, but on the other hand there was some attraction to the challenge that was impossible to ignore.

Not that I had any choice. Gerry Westenra, the New Zealander Commanding Officer, had a wealth of experience, having flown the old Gladiator biplanes in Greece early in the war against Me 109s. In addition, he proved to be a most congenial fellow, as was Richardson. We got along like a house on fire, and the squadron prospered. But I'm jumping ahead again.

There was one other interesting occurrence on the day we joined 93, although it was not nearly as important as the joining-up of the troops on the beach-head. In fact, it wasn't important at all. When we heard on the radio that Hitler had arranged a very bold rescue of his pal Mussolini from the latter's confinement in Northern Italy, we wondered what he would do with the pompous Fascist.

"Nothing," replied our C.O., who had spent years in the Mediterranean, "and since Italy has not only surrendered but also, apparently, come over to our side, I don't give a damn what the Fuehrer does with the Duce, as long as he doesn't send him back."

And that, while unofficial, seemed to adequately express the sentiments of 93 Squadron. At least it would do for the moment.

Focke-Wulf FW 190, an excellent Luftwaffe fighter aircraft.

Chapter VIII

Salerno Beach

(Ref. Map: Malta, Sicily and Italy)

It wasn't much of a move from 111 Squadron to 93 Squadron of the same wing. I never left the landing strip in the lemon grove at Falcone, on the northern coast of Sicily. I picked up the few belongings that I had taken with me to the Middle East, the rest having been stored in London about a year earlier. This amounted to a partly filled parachute bag. Those flexible zippered bags were designed to carry a parachute, but more commonly contained pilot's luggage. I walked diagonally across to the other side of the strip.

It was still very warm in Sicily on that September day, and I was dressed as lightly as possible: khaki shirt and shorts. The Adjutant met me and offered to send a Jeep over for my stuff. I had to tell him that I had it all with me.

He gave me a list of the pilots in the squadron, including, I noticed, one in sick bay with malaria. He showed me my tent which contained a camp cot with mosquito netting, and little else. That was about it for the Adj. I would meet the pilots and senior NCOs later. (The squadron had been relieved of duty for a day.) I told him that I would like to see the aircraft, and wandered out among the Spits dispersed in the lemon grove.

93 Squadron letters were HN, painted neatly on all of the aircraft, followed, as was the custom in all RAF squadrons, by another letter, A to M, for "A" flight, N to Z for "B". I didn't know what aircraft I would get, nor whether it would be a Spit V or IX. They didn't seem to be as far along in their change over to "Nines" as Treble-One Squadron, so perhaps I would have to revert to a "Five" for awhile. I reasoned that it would be somewhat difficult for a

Five to keep up to a Nine, but not vice-versa; it might be better for me, therefore, as flight commander to fly a Five.

The aircraft were clean and tidy, and I wondered why the squadron's morale was reported to be low. Probably there was nothing more to it than a lack of success against the Luftwaffe, plus the recent loss of several Spitfires and pilots through mistaken identity at the beachhead.

The list of pilots which the Adjutant had given to me seemed to be rather typical of an RAF squadron at that time. A New Zealander was C.O., with fifteen pilots in "A" Flight and fourteen in "B", of whom seven were Canadians, two Australian, four New Zealanders, and the rest British. Commissioned and non-commissioned pilots were almost equally represented. I thought that it was going to be an interesting job without too much responsibility. I was twenty-one, and I'm afraid I was a little selfish about my independence. I did not want the job to interfere with my freedom to shoot down Huns, which I still considered to be my main preoccupation. On the other hand, I was ready to have a good crack at it, and do the best I could.

The next morning we were airborne, my first flight with 93, heading across the Tyrrhenian Sea for Salerno Beach, with long range fuel tanks. I was flying a Spit VIII, an excellent aircraft so similar to a IX that I didn't notice any difference. It was supercharged with the same series of Merlin engine as the IX, and had a maximum level speed of 416 mph. Actually, the Spit VIII was supposed to replace the Five, and the Nine initially was a stop-gap. But the Nine had proven to be one of those rare aircraft that are "right" in so many ways, that it became the dominant Spitfire until the end of the war.

I was leading the flight toward the south end of the beach-head, when the ground station reported "bandits" over Salerno beach. We were at 19,000 feet over Agropoli, when I saw four Focke-Wulf 190s about four miles north at 15,000 feet, just rolling over to dive bomb some shipping close to the shore. At least I presumed by their action that they were Focke-Wulfs.

Quick response was essential. I asked Yellow One to take over the patrol of the beach-head. I jettisoned my long range tank, stuck the nose down, opened the throttle, and cut the angle on the Focke-Wulfs, knowing that they would be diving out to the north-east. I presumed that my number Two would come with me. That was customary, but not, apparently, at 93. Anyway, there was a misunderstanding, and I was alone.

I pursued the FW 190s for fifty miles or a little more, over the Apennine backbone ridge of the country to the plains on the east side of Italy. One of the FW 190s had apparently become separated because, when I caught up to them and they turned on me, there were only three. And it was at that time that I realized I was alone.

It may seem untrue, or at least an exaggeration if I say that I was not afraid, but that's the way it was. I remember exactly what crossed my mind when I found myself among the three 190s. Quite calmly I thought to myself, "The next few minutes are going to be very interesting." I may well have been over-confident, but if so, it was a good thing. Confidence was essential in this game. By this time I was so used to a Spitfire that I was part of it, or it was an extension of me. Strapped in tightly, it didn't matter in the least what position one was in. Upside down was as compatible as right side up, properly tied in. It was left hand on the throttle, right hand on the stick, feet on the rudder pedals, and thumb on the gun button. Then the idea was to push and abuse the qualities of the aircraft, and force my own stamina, both to the maximum. If there had to be a war, surely this was the way it should be fought, this clean, unrestrained, impersonal duel. And for exactly four years, a war had been necessary. Had there ever been a war in which the issues were so clearly defined?

With the comfortable confidence from unity with my aircraft, my emotion was not fear, but excitement. The stimulation always arrived simultaneously with the black crosses off my wingtip.

I knew that the Focke-Wulf 190 was an excellent aircraft of approximately the same performance as a Spitfire IX, but with different characteristics. It could not turn as tightly nor climb as quickly, both of which were expressions of lift. But it could dive and zoom, flick-roll and short flick-turn more rapidly than a Spitfire. In this it resembled an Me 109, but it had more power than the Messerschmitt. I preferred our characteristics, but the advantage, by those who discussed it, was generally considered to boil down to whichever pilot got the jump. I was quite confident, however, that I had the advantage in a Spit IX (or on this day, a Spit VIII), if the other fellow would stay and fight.

I must say that I was not particularly concerned about the fact that there were three Focke-Wulf 190s here, because in my experience, when one engaged the leader of the flight, the other pilots tended to circle around the periphery and not get involved. They seemed to respect the leader's prerogative. I don't know whether this was a general Luftwaffe tendency, and I don't recall ever discussing it with the fellows, but it was definitely the way I felt they behaved.

This time however, I was closing in on one 190 when another one turned on me and I was involved with both of them for a couple of minutes. At that point, one of my cannons jammed. I was left with four machine guns and one cannon, the recoil from which caused the aircraft to yaw sideways. Then the two FW 190s followed their customary behaviour and circled around the periphery while their leader and I had (what we called) a good go at it.

I think that this fellow was a very experienced pilot and perhaps the best that I had ever encountered up to that time. He absolutely refused to fight in a way that would allow me to utilize the Spitfire's superior qualities. In short, he would not stay with me because he knew that I could turn a tighter radius and get on his tail, and it would be all over. He fought entirely his way, and I couldn't do a thing about it. This consisted of a series of shallow dives at full speed, zooming up, flick-turning, and coming back at me, head-on. I would meet him head-on, then whip the Spit around tightly to port as he was going by, with full throttle the whole time, watch him zoom up out of range and flick-turn around to come down at me again, by which time, of course, I would have completed my tight turn.

Sometimes I got a short burst head-on. But I acknowledge that with the long nose of the Spitfire, it was difficult to pull on the little bit of deflection that was necessary without losing the Focke-Wulf under the nose, and presenting a target. So some of these short bursts were pure intimidation just before he would zoom by my wingtip.

I had never worked so hard in a scrap. My aircraft behaved very well (other than the jammed cannon) as I jerked it around mercilessly, pulling back as hard as I could on the stick, producing so much G-force that my mouth fell open every turn: the masseter muscles were overcome by gravity force and I couldn't keep my jaws clenched shut. This meant that after each turn I had to reach up and pull my oxygen mask down again when my lower jaw got below it. No problem, but inconvenient.

"Damn you," I swore. "Why won't you stay with me?"

But I knew the answer. And I knew that he knew, and that's all there was to it. Well, almost all.

Finally, I got a fair lick at him and saw strikes, and a piece of his sheet metal tore off and fell away like a leaf in the wind. My first impression was that it was a piece of the cowling, but I didn't see any smoke or fire. Focke-Wulfs were formidable. Air-cooled engines had no radiators for glycol leaks. Then I wondered if he had just jettisoned a slip tank. But he couldn't have because he had been bombing and couldn't carry both, and in any case I would have seen an external tank. Certainly, the other two Focke-Wulfs which I was watching out of the corner of my eye did not have drop tanks. So it must have been sheet metal.

Anyway, I lost him. We were down near the ground when two more FW 190s in fairly close formation appeared from the east, probably Foggia, and

I thought it prudent to leave: I was a long way from home. I left the throttle open for a few minutes, but didn't see any of the Focke-Wulfs following.

I headed west toward Salerno Beach. Just that day we had been informed that an emergency strip was available for refuelling. I found it close to the beach, and set the Spit down amidst artillery flashes alongside the strip. It seemed more hazardous than my argument with the 190s.

I saw American troops lining up with mess tins at a big marquee, so I got in line and in no time had a couple of wieners and catsup and potatoes. I hadn't seen wieners for two and a half years, and they were good. It is surprising how tasty a simple food becomes when it has been unavailable for a long time. Our rations in Malta were based upon Argentinian corned beef – good basic food, but daily variety was limited to how the cook prepared it. Hence the feast of a dozen fresh eggs in Sicily, and the wieners at Salerno. By the time I ate, my aircraft was refuelled, and I got away.

It was just under an hour of easy flying from Salerno Beach back to Sicily. When I taxied up to 93's dispersal, the two mechanics responsible for my aircraft ran out to meet me. I hadn't seen that enthusiasm for quite awhile: they were elated to see their aircraft with the patches blown off the guns. I hadn't really done well. I should have clobbered that damned 190. But it looked as though the ground crew's morale had got a lift, and I suppose that was worth something.

* * * *

With the landing of more British and American troops on the bridge-head in Italy, and the link-up of the Eighth Army from the south with the forces on the beach, on September 18th the Germans began their withdrawal northwards from Salerno. Five days later, our wing moved to Montecorvino on the bridge-head. We were in Italy. Ninety-gallon long range tanks were forgotten. Although we sometimes still used thirty-gallon slip tanks to increase our endurance, most of the time we were on short hops. We were covering the American Fifth Army's push north of Naples, while 322 Spitfire Wing supported the British Eighth Army, including the First Canadian Division, on the Adriatic side of Italy. There they captured the airfields at Foggia, so recently occupied by the Luftwaffe.

By early October, the Fifth and Eighth Armies had established a continuous line across Italy (only 120 miles long) along the Volturno River, north of Naples, and the Biferno River which flows into the Adriatic at Termoli. The western end of this line was to occupy us for many months.

Meanwhile sunny Sicily was forgotten while it poured rain at Salerno, and our aircraft were mired in the mud at Battipaglia. When the water ran six inches deep through the tents, we learned why trenches were dug around them. I visited the army and got an excellent pair of British army boots, waterproof, comfortable, and good for flying. I found a steel single bed with a mattress in an abandoned house, and took it back to my tent. It was much better than a camp cot in the mud. We only missed a couple of days flying, hauled the aircraft onto dry land, and got airborne again. Me 109s jumped a section over the beach, and we lost young Flight Sergeant Crist, but we more than held our own.

On October 11th, we left Salerno Beach and moved up to Capodichino airport at Naples. This was a large grass airport and was much superior to a strip in the rainy season. We packed our tents and moved indoors, into one of the hundreds of abandoned villas of the wealthy. We learned that close behind the advancing army, a bit of looting, while never officially condoned, could be done — and had been done since Hannibal and Caesar had marched around the Mediterranean. While the vast majority of the population had remained in Naples, that small proportion of wealthy Neapolitans had disappeared northwards during the upheaval. At least we presumed they had fled: the villas were all empty. But they had left their cars behind because of fuel shortage. So every squadron picked up a few cars and a motorcycle or two which ran very nicely on hundred octane aircraft fuel, until the authorities stopped the practice.

Whilst our job, by definition, kept us high and dry, our unfortunate confrères in the army faced a long slog in the mud of the Volturno and Garigliano Rivers in the west, and the Sangro and Moro Rivers on the Adriatic side of Italy. Kesselring had assured Hitler that a line across the central mountain ridge, requiring concentrated defence only at each end on the Mediterranean and Adriatic flanks, could be held almost indefinitely. This bitter and costly winter campaign now began for the Allies. This fight in the Apennines has been described as "the bitterest and bloodiest of [the Allied] struggles with the Wehrmacht on any front of the Second World War."[1]

---

(1)
   *John Keegan in **The Second World War***

Chapter IX
North of Naples

In October, 1943, we were quite happy to be based at Capodichino aerodrome in the suburbs of Naples. There was no place that we would rather be. It was not that the city of Naples had any attraction; we never went into town. It was flying close support to the Allied armies in their impossibly difficult task against Kesselring's defence that presented the challenge. This was what we had trained for, and we were sure to have more fun than the fellows back in England who were impatiently awaiting the second front in Europe. The Normandy invasion would not materialize for another eight months. So this was the place to be flying Spitfires at this particular time, and we were enthusiastic.

The place was steeped in history. Within sight of the aerodrome was volcanic Mount Vesuvius, about eight miles away, with the remains of Pompeii at its base. About fifty miles north of Naples was Monte Cassino, the great fortress abbey where Saint Benedict had established the roots of European monasticism 1400 years earlier. And seventy miles north of Cassino was Rome itself. Our Wing Commander, tall, lanky, red-haired Cocky Dundas,seemed to like to take us up around Rome on Sunday mornings. It was exciting to look down at the place where Julius Caesar had been, and to see the dome of St. Peter's.

But Cocky was looking for Messerschmitt 109s. He was naturally irreverent. He called the Huns all kinds of names and challenged them to come up. We enjoyed these trips; they were good for morale.

After the Salerno Beach success, the Allies drove north to attack Kesselring's winter position, the western end of which was known as the Gustav Line. This hinged on the Monte Cassino fortress which proved to be impregnable for several months. But first the Fifth Army had to establish bridge-heads across the Volturno River about twenty miles north of Naples. They did this between October 12th and 15th, and it was our job to support them. When we were not escorting bombers, we had to control the air over the front so that the troops were not harassed. Volturno patrols went on all day long, and this meant that each of us flew a couple of times a day. We found the Huns were out in force.

October 13th was a fine day with a bit of cumulus cloud at 8,000 feet. I was Packard Red One, airborne at 1105 hours leading a section of Spitfires of 93 Squadron, patrolling over the Volturno River.

At 14,000 feet, I saw two aircraft north of us which looked like Me 109s. We pursued these, but they were decoys. We knew that old Luftwaffe trick and we were watching our tails when inevitably more Me 109s attacked us from the rear. We broke around into them and spoiled their advantage; then it was even. After a couple of tight turns, I got on the tail of a 109 but before I could get a shot off, he rolled over and dove vertically nearly to ground level. He pulled away from me with his superior diving speed. I had only a Spit V, but it was a good "Five". In any case one can only dive so far, and the 109 levelled off at about 500 feet, heading north. I chased him flat out for twenty miles and caught him near Marzano. I hit him a good clout in the port radiator and engine. The pilot baled out promptly, but for some reason, perhaps a moment of terror when he felt the Spitfire's cannons ripping into his aircraft, or perhaps because his controls were damaged, he neglected to pull up a little. It was a fatal error. He was too low. When he hit the ground with his forward momentum of 300 mph, he bounced two or three times like a rubber ball, just as his parachute was opening.

"That Hun was in an awful hurry to get out, Red One." It was Red Two, a Scot named Jock, who had stayed with me through the chase.

"That's the wrong way to do it, Jock," I answered, then called up the other fellows who had got stuck into the 109s.

"Packard Red Section, Red One here," I called. "Reform over mouth of Volturno River at 8,000 feet. Over."

Red Two and I climbed back south, and when approaching the Volturno at 8,000 feet I saw twelve more Me 109s diving down from the port rear quarter. It wasn't hard to see them; they were not up-sun. They were easy to count, three sections of four. It was unusual for twelve 109s to attack 'en masse' two Spitfires, but here they came.

"Packard Red Two, break port now twelve 109s!" I yelled as I pulled around hard to meet the 109s head on. The 109s went through us and pulled up around to port. In the mêlée that followed, Jock lost me. I remained in a full bore climb, circling to port. I don't think that the Huns ever completely broke formation, but remained in three separate fours, following each other around me. They were flying rather mechanically, and after the initial pass, I didn't see any firing. As long as they remained in three finger-four[1] sections in this climbing turn following me around, I could see them all and count the three fours again and again.

The three sections of Messerschmitts and my Spitfire were evenly spaced around the circle to port, with the middle section of four 109s exactly opposite me. I knew that I had a little better climb even in a Spit V, and certainly in this turn with full throttle I had the advantage over the twelve 109s as long as the dolts remained in three sections. It's absolutely impossible to climb a section of aircraft in a turn as quickly as a single aircraft, because the guy on

---

(1)

A finger-four section was so called because the four aircraft flew almost abreast, like looking at the back of your finger tips spread apart (ignoring the thumb). The tails of the two aircraft on the left were covered by the cross vision of the two aircraft on the right, and vise-versa. This formation, originated by the Luftwaffe, was introduced to the RAF by our Wing Commander, Cocky Dundas, in 1941. It was much superior to the old line astern formation of the Battle of Britain, and was readily adaptable to eight or twelve aircraft (two or three fours).

the outside of the turn can't keep up unless the leader throttles back. So I began to feel rather comfortable, and certainly alert. At 16,000 feet, I had gained 1,000 feet on the twelve 109s, still turning in the same radius. They were playing it my way. I called up on the R/T.

"Packard Red One here to any aircraft in the area. I am over the mouth of the Volturno at sixteen thousand with twelve 109s. Over."

My old squadron, Treble One, promptly answered. They knew my voice, and were coming on patrol.

"Banker Blue One here. Hold them, Hap. We're coming."

I thought this was hilarious, and called back.

"Banker Blue. How do you propose that I hold twelve 109s?" I thought of a story that had made the rounds. Some joker had got caught with a squadron of twelve 109s and had called up for help: "I've got them surrounded," he said.

111 Squadron called twice more to say they were coming full speed, but it was immaterial now because the 109s started to dive gently out to the north, one section after the other. I watched them all go, and circled once more; no sign of any Spitfire or Messerschmitt.

I thought that I might as well follow them discreetly as I knew their habits and I figured that only three or four of these guys were experienced. Usually 109s going home dove down to about 1,000 feet, sometimes less, and kept a lot of throttle on for about thirty miles. It appeared that these fellows might follow the pattern. I dove down full throttle to near ground level, and followed the dozen spots which were a mile ahead of me. I counted them again. Three fours.

All fighter aircraft are blind behind and below, but especially Me 109s. That's exactly where I was – behind and below – and they couldn't see me unless they turned around, so I was quite comfortable. I was gaining slowly and waiting for them to throttle back. This would be obvious by the cessation of black exhaust, following which I would gain very quickly.

This happened as expected. I gained quickly and was soon almost underneath them, looking up at the three fours. I was just about within range (our guns were harmonized at 250 yards) and feeling once again that tremendous exhilaration of anticipation, when the Messerschmitts most obligingly began to move into tight formation. I could hardly believe my good luck, because when aircraft move into tight formation they are so intent upon looking at each other that no one looks behind.

It also meant just one thing: we were approaching their base and they were putting on a show for their ground crew. I looked straight ahead, and sure enough, there it was – a large grass airfield.

"Thank you very much, you clots," I said to myself, remembering that we had been taught never to fly in tight formation in a war zone.

One Messerschmitt was a little slow moving in. It was always this way. We called him "Arse-end Charlie." I pulled up from ground level and joined the formation behind Charlie. I'm sure that all the ground crews watched the elliptical winged Spitfire join the tapered wing 109s, because we were right at the edge of the airfield when I got Charlie in my sights and fired.

Damn! My starboard cannon jammed, and the Spitfire yawed hard to port due to the recoil of the port cannon. I missed the 109 completely. Still the squadron of 109s remained in tight formation. I quickly compensated, aiming off to the right, fired again, and this time saw a very good cannon strike, a large flash.

"I got him!" I said to myself, and I swung the Spit around hard to starboard in a flat-out climb. Looking over my right shoulder in the turn I saw a parachute floating down toward the green field. I was not going to press my luck any further; my best move was a maximum climb due south. I felt absolutely elated.

"How do you like that, you bloody Huns?" I thought. They had done everything wrong.

Although I would have been happier in a Spit IX, I was not worried about their catching me in a climb, full throttle, 3,000 RPM., 165 mph, indicating 3,750 feet per minute climb, and I never looked back. I went through some cumulus at 8,000 feet, and only then turned slightly and looked below. There was no sign of any aircraft popping up through the white clouds, and I eased back on the throttle. I continued back to the Volturno River where I picked up Red Three and Four again, and resumed patrol until we returned to base at 1220. There we found Red Two, who thought that I had gone down when the twelve attacked.

Our AOC in Italy at the time was Air Vice-Marshal Harry Broadhurst. He was a superb commander, as he had been an excellent wing leader at Hornchurch years earlier. I never met him, but we all knew of him. I was told that some senior officer (I do not know if it was the AOC) on being informed of my adventure with the twelve Me 109s, said that it was "a likely story," insinuating that it lacked credibility. Whoever it was that questioned it, did so quite legitimately, and I did not blame him in the least. Indeed, he should have done so. It was certainly unusual for one Spitfire to follow twelve Me 109s home. No doubt some would call it foolish, but at the time I thought it perfectly reasonable, a unique opportunity. Turning back prematurely never crossed my mind. Of course, I could not confirm it. I was alone, and we had no camera guns at that time in Italy to record our claims. And in the insouciance of youth, it didn't matter in the least whether high officials believed me.

To some degree, it was the same easy attitude with which I was able to ignore being shot at by another Spitfire earlier in Malta. This adventure with the 109s, culminating as it did over the Luftwaffe's aerodrome and witnessed by their ground crew, was a more than adequate end in itself. It had not been undertaken for reward or applause. Respectfully, I didn't give a damn what H.Q. thought.[2]

(2)

Regarding the two combats with 109s on October 13, the first one twenty miles north of the mouth of the Volturno River, and the second a few miles further north in the lower Liri Valley, Christopher Shores, air war historian of London, England, reports in private corrspondence dated 25 February, 1992:

"13 October 1943: Your opponents were from III/Jagdgeschwader 77 (Bf 109 fighters). Oberleutnant Helmut Hansel, the 9 Staffel Kapitan was killed west of Teano in 'Yellow 9'. Unteroffizier Hans-Werner Maximow of 9 Staffel baled out of 'Yellow 13' in the same general area. Feldwebel Walter Stammwitz of 8 Staffel was missing north-west of Capua in 'Black 6'. A fourth of the unit's aircraft was hit and crash landed, all reportedly in combat with Spitfires. "The ONLY Allied claims on this date were made by 93 Squadron, two Bf 109s (yourself) and Flying Officer Davidson with one probable, from a reported sixteen over the Volturno River. My impression would be that you got the two 9 Staffel aircraft."

Thus, finally, an "unlikely story" of 13 October 1943 is confirmed some forty-eight years later, with the name of Hans-Werner Maximow, the pilot of the Me 109 who baled out of 'Yellow 13" over the lovely green lower Liri Valley. The grass airfield was probably Aquino, close to Monte Cassino.

Messerschmitt Bf 109 of JG 53. Note Ace of Spades on engine cowling. We saw a lot of the Ace of Spades Squadron, from Africa to Italy.

Mechanics Bill Hollis and Ken Pickering with their aircraft and pilot at Capodichino.

Dawn at Capodichino, Naples, with Mt. Vesuvius smoking in the background.

Chapter X
Monte Cassino

While the Fifth Army was establishing bridgeheads across the Volturno River, we continued our daily patrols overhead. We ran into Me 109s intermittently; I think that the 109s were there, as we were, every day, but sometimes the other squadrons in the wing engaged them and some days we missed them entirely.

On October 15th, I was Packard Blue One leading a section over the bridgehead at 12,000 feet when we saw eight 109s above and behind us, coming down. We turned and faced them and got right into them quickly. One crossed in front of me in a climbing turn to starboard. I pulled up hard behind him, close to the stall, and got a quick deflection shot from the right rear quarter. I saw my cannon shells explode around the cockpit. The Messerschmitt caught fire at once and fell away. With all the traffic, I did not look down, but my number two confirmed that the 109 went into a spiral dive and disappeared on fire into the cloud below.

Less than two minutes had elapsed. But more Messerschmitts had arrived and there was a lot of yelling "Break" this way or that way, as an Me was seen on a Spit's tail.

I saw three 109s from this second group diving down toward the cloud below. I circled once to make sure that there were no more around, then I rolled over and went down through the clouds vertically with full throttle where I had seen the three disappear. Usually the 109s dove out at high speed, but this time my estimate of their speed was all wrong, made worse by the fact that while I had previously been flying Spit Fives, on this day I had a IX. Another two hundred and fifty horses made a big difference. It was an old "Nine" that had somehow come to us from maintenance. It had a Polish insignia, a red and white chequer about eight inches square on the cowl just in front of the cockpit. No doubt it had been flown by one of the Polish pilots of 145 Squadron in the other wing. And Polish pilots hated the Huns with an intensity that only someone whose homeland has been invaded could comprehend. Consequently, they beat their aircraft mercilessly, and this old Nine was very loose and not pretty.

Anyway, it was nobody's fault but my own that I broke through the bottom of the stratocumulus going far too fast, and had to pull hard to starboard to avoid collision with the 109s. I had no chance to get a shot away. I had spoiled the whole exercise; all surprise was gone. The only thing I noticed when I dodged them was that the 109 in the center, the leader, did not have wing cannons like the other two. I could have pulled back up, I had so much speed, but I thought now that I had arrived, I might as well have a crack at these guys. I had closed the throttle automatically when I first broke upon them, but that was futile – there were no air brakes. So I opened it again and pulled around to starboard to find the leader without the underslung cannons ready to take me on.

This fellow was a very experienced 109 pilot, and knew the qualities of my Spitfire. Like the Focke-Wulf pilot of Salerno Beach, he refused to stay and turn with me. He dived, zoomed, climbed up out of range, then flick-turned to come back head-on, keeping his speed up. I beat the old Spit IX as hard as I could, full throttle the whole time, pulling back with all my strength in tight turns when the 109 went by my wingtip, losing my vision in temporary blackout due to the gravity force, then easing the control column slightly to get it back in time to see the 109 flick-turn around and return in head-on attack.[1]

------

(1)
> *It was quite a common experience. And there was nothing complicated about easing into and out of blackout. One did not lose consciousness, only vision, by pulling back hard on the control column and increasing the "G" force and decreasing the blood supply to the brain. One's vision would return again as soon as one eased forward on the control column.*

This went on for quite a long time. We had gradually dropped down to perhaps 500 feet above the hilltops. Neither of us could gain an edge on the other; each was using the best characteristics of his aircraft. I was annoyed at my carelessness in overshooting these three birds; it should have been easy picking. I was not concerned with the two 109s with the underslung cannons. We knew that the better pilots didn't like the extra weight, didn't need the extra cannons (they already had one in the nose), and preferred the better manoeuvrability. So these two were rookies and to hell with them. But something had to give soon!

Then it happened. I jerked the Spit around harder than ever as we were getting down near the ground. There was a loud explosion, and a tremendous blast of air into the cockpit blew dust and small bits and pieces of debris into my face. I couldn't see much but concluded that one of the other 109s had clobbered me behind the cockpit armour-plating. Certainly the leader had not got a shot at me, but I had been largely ignoring the other two, and perhaps the leader had talked to them. The controls all seemed to be intact, but I didn't know how long they would last. There might be a frayed cable, and ground-level was no place to lose control. I pulled the nose up, and watched the three 109s turn north and disappear.

My engine was behaving fine. I slowed the aircraft to a near-stall, and the controls seemed normal. The dirt settled, but there was a terrible draught. The radio was dead. I went back to the Volturno and picked up Packard Blue Section, and we returned to Capodichino.

The landing gear and flaps came down fine. The mechanics had already spotted the large square opening in the port side of the fuselage, and were waiting when I taxied in.

It turned out that my aircraft had not been hit by the enemy. Our radios were rigged with explosives that were designed to destroy the radio and IFF (Identification Friend or Foe) on crash landing, to prevent their falling into German hands. In my final violent manoeuvre, I had blown up the radio and door on the fuselage with it. I had never previously heard of such a thing happening, and it was the first time that the chief N.C.O. had seen it. So it had not been necessary to break off that scrap after all, and that was disappointing. I suppose it could be called a draw, and there was nothing I could do about it. But I had been lucky when the first 109 made a mistake and crossed in front of me, and in that scrap, three of the boys, Browne (New Zealand), Hockey (Canada), and Davidson (Britain) had each got an Me 109. We hadn't lost anyone. 93 Squadron had done well;[2] under Squadron Leader Westenra we led the Wing in enemy aircraft destroyed in the month of October.

There was a friendly rivalry among the five squadrons, which was perhaps most evident among the ground crew. 93's dramatic recovery in morale in only one month was obvious among the pilots, but more particularly when the ground crew ran out to meet us, enquire about the aircraft's performance, and smartly refuel and rearm.

The mechanics cleaned up the interior of my old Spit, and found a new door and a new radio. Most of the dirt was minuscule remnants of the previous radio. No wonder I had been unable to see for a moment.

* * * *

---

(2)

Christopher Shores in private correspondence dated 25 February, 1992, reports:"15 October, 1943: 93 Squadron saw eight Bf 109s over the Volturno and claimed four destroyed. 111 Squadron in the same area reported thirty plus Bf 109s and FW 190s and claimed one destroyed and three damaged. Luftwaffe losses were four Bf 109s and one FW 190. Two of the Bf 109 pilots from I/JG77 who were shot down by Spitfires, survived unhurt. There were NO OTHER Allied fighter claims on this date."

The Fifth Army got across the Volturno and continued slogging northward to the Garigliano River, from which the valley of the Liri led past Monte Cassino toward Rome. But this valley was dominated by almost impregnable mountain peaks including Cassino itself, which had to be bombed before the army could consider assault.

Our patrols changed to bomber escorts of Fortresses, Baltimores, and frequently three squadrons of Bostons at a time. We escorted up to nine squadrons of fighter-bomber Mustangs and Kittyhawks against the German mountain positions. We strafed transports north of the line, but there wasn't a lot of it in daylight, and flying in the mountain valleys was dangerous when strafing. One tended to concentrate on the strafing and lose the perspective of the steep mountains.

One day I had to pull back with all my strength to avoid the roadside trees, and before I could warn the young lad behind me, he had flown through the trees and pulled up with no wing whatever on one side of his Spitfire. He didn't get out. Two transports and one staff car cost one Spitfire and Stan Swain.

But air power had its limitations in the Italian topography. We couldn't find the defenders behind the steep rocky hillsides. We sometimes chased but could not catch Focke-Wulf 190s with Spit Fives; the fellows with the Nines did.

I had a couple of days off in mid November, and set off in my old Fiat to visit the front. About twelve miles north of Naples, I found myself trapped in a large convoy of American stake bodied trucks loaded with food. We were poking along. I had my window open when I heard an aircraft overhead, then another. I knew that they were not ours; there was no Spitfire whistle. Then a Focke-Wulf roared by my window and the strafing started. The convoy stopped and the drivers jumped out into a shallow ditch. Because the 190s were strafing down the road and not across it, I stayed in the car, protected by the trucks. The stake body on the truck in front of me was well splintered and grapefruit juice started squirting out in all directions. It was like a ruddy fountain, and I started to laugh. It was over pretty quickly, and I sat down on the side of the ditch. The friendly truck driver, obviously from the South, handed me a can of grapefruit juice with a hole in it.

"Would y'all like a drink?" he asked. "Don't need no can opener."

I thanked him. Only Americans would carry grapefruit juice 3,500 miles to their troops.

There wasn't much harm done to the convoy. An Italian on a bicycle was killed, however. After waiting a couple of hours, I decided to go back to Naples and try another day. I felt frustrated at seeing those Focke-Wulfs from such a helpless position. It was hard to find them in the air, but here they were. Maybe we were flying too high.

Sometimes we were on the receiving end of bombing and strafing in Naples. One night during an air raid (it was November second) we were looking down the street at the fireworks from the upstairs open windows of the villa. A Junkers 88 came roaring down the road just above the rooftops, firing its guns, apparently indiscriminately. Freddie Mellors of 111 Squadron leaned heavily on a couple of lads and they pushed him off. He slumped to the floor without a word. He was dead. The 88 had hit him in the neck. It was a poor way for a fighter pilot to die.

The RAF had established an aircrew rest camp at Sorrento near the Isle of Capri. Perhaps it would be more accurate to say that a hotel which had recently been a rest camp for Luftwaffe pilots had been taken over by the RAF. It was close by, and some of us were sent over for a few days. I was amused by the apparent ability of the Italian staff to adapt to changing circumstances. They quickly converted from German to British rations, while the violins played the same beautiful music among the tables that they had played to the Luftwaffe three weeks earlier. And no doubt the musicians had made the same polite bow from the waist, with "Si Signor." Such benign pacificism was a little difficult for us to understand, and impossible to embrace. But we enjoyed the white table cloths, the silver and the violins. Civilized etiquette was still alive, if somewhat hard to find. I only stayed two days and thought that I had better get back to the flight. Perhaps that was an indication that I should have stayed longer. In any case, the beautiful song "Sorrento" has remained a favourite of mine ever since.

I went back up to the front at the Garigliano River for two and a half days, and saw grim reality. The soldiers lived, at this time of the year, in the mud of the river valleys that were dominated by the surrounding mountain peaks. There would be no progress up the Liri valley until each mountain peak, including Monte Cassino, was scaled and captured. I thought that it was a terribly formidable prospect, yet the lads were cheery and ready to have a crack at it. I felt an empathy with the soldiers. I did not envy them their job, but a young Captain told me that he preferred to have his feet on the ground, and if it were muddy this time of the year, so be it.

I recalled discussing war at sea with the First Lieutenant of the Royal Navy sloop HMS "Erne" during a convoy to North Africa in the fall of 1942. In spite of the cold North Atlantic, the U-boats, and the discomfort of a small rolling ship, those fellows would not trade their job for the army or the air. So no matter which service one was in, it seemed that we could adapt to it, and it boiled down to a lot of training, familiarity, considerable luck while one gained experience, and finally competence. And with competence, fear disappeared or at least became irrelevant, and each of us was quite content with his job. And until the evil ambitions of Hitler were overcome, our present work was precisely what we wanted to do.

After my visit to the army, I flew with renewed vigour. I dropped down a little lower over the army boys at the Garigliano River to show our support, and picked up some pretty accurate flak from the Huns. We escorted bombers to Cassino, Frosinone and Aquino. We strafed transports and went back again to the Garigliano, and got more flak.

It never crossed my mind that I might be getting tired. But one of the pilots complained to the C.O. that I was paying no attention whatever to flak, and one day in December, Squadron Leader Westenra called me in. He asked me if it were true that I had been severely rocked by heavy flak and had continued on course.

I laughed and said, "I guess so. It didn't bother me."

"That's the point exactly," Gerry replied. "It should have bothered you enough to provoke violent evasive action. I'm standing you down, right now. You're away overdue. I don't know whether it will be the U.K. or Cairo, but there'll be no more ops for six months."

Gerry was a most reasonable fellow. He seemed to have made up his mind. There was nothing left for me to say. I felt a little bit empty.

Chapter XI
Normandy

(Ref. Map: Normandy 1)

Only a day or two after I was taken off operational flying, I realized that the C.O. was right, and in fact I had a good chuckle about it. "Stand down" was usually and ideally done in RAF squadrons before any symptoms of operational fatigue occurred. The routine time in Fighter Command was 200 operational flying hours. In Bomber Command thirty trips, each of six or seven hours, amounted to the same thing, though their casualties were higher than ours.

The commonest minor symptoms of fatigue were irritability and insomnia. But the most obvious give-away when a fellow remained on ops a little too long (especially in Malta), was what was known as "the twitch." This was an involuntary muscle contraction, usually of the head, sometimes of an upper or lower limb. When this happened, the individual would try to hide it. But someone in the dispersal would soon spot it, jump up and point mercilessly at the victim and yell "Twitch! twitch!" until, joined by others, the whole dispersal was yelling and laughing. The victim would appeal "Sit down, you silly bastards!" to no avail. Enter the C.O. "What's going on here?"

Everyone: "Joe's got the twitch!"
Joe, angrily: "I bloody well haven't got the bloody twitch."
But usually he "bloody well" had, and he was shipped out smartly.

Sometimes one's flying behaviour was the clue to fatigue, and strangely enough it took two extremes. Some fellows didn't want to fly anymore, but neither did they want to acknowledge it. Instead they found minor faults with their aircraft. For others, the exact opposite applied: completely relaxed nonchalance, a sort of "Get me if you can, you bastards!" I had fallen into this latter group; I wasn't at all concerned about enemy flak, and got careless. It was not appreciated.

A week before Christmas, 1943, a DC 3 took a dozen of us from Naples over to Tunis to the Base Personnel Depot. I knew a few of the fellows proceeding on the "rest": S.F. "Brownie" Brown, a New Zealander, Ross Whitney and Bill Olmsted from Ontario, and Bill Hockey from Nova Scotia. There were also a number of pilots from the various Spitfire wings in Italy (the Malta Wing had joined 322, 244 and 324 Wings) who had recently been ill with malaria and hepatitis, and were now on their way back to England.

In Tunis, Bill, Ross, Brownie and I, with nothing to do, enjoyed daily brisk walks in the city. We should have gone out to the ruins of Hannibal's Carthage to look at the remnants of a much earlier war, but couldn't manage it. Tourism did not exist. What struck me most forcibly about Tunis were the disease and disability. Every few yards on the street, one encountered the blind and lepers, cripples of all ages, unfortunates with open sores sitting on the pavement rattling tin cups for a few pennies. All were dressed in rags, many with opaque unseeing eyes, while one-legged children hobbling on sticks kicked at a soccer ball. These were not war casualties; they were the poor, "the halt, the lame and the blind who are always with us" in these countries. The vision of them stayed with me. Surely they deserved more than a tin cup.

After a couple of weeks, we learned with some relief that we would be going back to England, and we flew west from Tunis to the port city of Algiers. The weather was fair and, even though it was mid-winter, mild enough for us to swim on the North African coast. We began to feel relaxed, but only slowly did we adapt to the realization that we were not going to fly this day. The pace of everything seemed deliberately slow though no doubt it was normal troop movement.

On January 18, we embarked on S.S. Elizabethville, a Belgian ship, for Great Britain. Four days later we stopped at Gibraltar for a day, then joined a convoy to the U.K. The pleasant stateroom, modest variety of food, and leisurely pace of the voyage had a salutary effect upon our highstrung minds. We docked at Greenock in Scotland on February 4th, my twenty-second birthday. We took the night train down to Bournemouth on the south coast, where a number of luxurious pre-war beach hotels had been designated as RCAF holding centres.

I knew that my younger brother, Carleton, had arrived in England, but I had no idea where he was. It was, to say the least, a pleasant coincidence when I found myself standing behind him in the cafeteria of the Royal Bath Hotel. I let him sit down at a table, with his tray, before I said "G'day Tot," using the familiar name we had always called him since he had been a little tot. It was nearly three years since I had seen him; he had stretched from a small teen to over six feet. He was commissioned, a member of a bomber crew of seven who were all there and awaiting posting to an Operational Training Unit.

It was good to see him and to get news from home. Not yet 21, he was only sixteen months younger than I, and we had grown up very close. Even in February, the weather on the south coast of England is gentle; we had some pleasant walks and talks.

Shortly thereafter, I requested a posting to the Central Gunnery School and was pleased to be accepted. The course was excellent; if one followed the instructions, one would certainly become a better shot. Following the classroom theory, they gave us old Spitfires with which we attacked from every possible angle twenty foot drogues towed by Lysanders.

At this time I was surprised to hear from Gerry Westenra, my recent Commanding Officer in Italy. He had returned to England and was now C.O. of a Mustang squadron at Gravesend, Kent, in preparation for the Second Front in France. He asked me to join him, which was very kind of him and gratifying for me, and I told him that I would love to. It would have been most interesting (the Mustang was an exceptional fighter aircraft), but H.Q. Air Defence of Great Britain would have none of it until my six months of non-operational flying were up. I later read that Gerry got a couple of Junkers 88s in 65 Squadron.

Toward the end of April, I finished the gunnery course and was sent as an instructor to Eastchurch, Kent, in the Thames estuary. Kent, in cherry blossom season must be about as close to heaven as one can ever get. It was absolutely beautiful for anyone who had the slightest appreciation of nature, and for the next month, in spite of the hundreds of Flying Fortresses of the United States Eighth Air Force daily flying over this south-east corner of England en route to Germany, the war seemed far away. I walked through the lanes and the fields in May, enjoyed the smell of the clover as only a country man can, lay down in it, looked at the blue sky, and savoured the skylark's song on the wing.

I knew, of course, that it was too good to last. We all knew that the second front, the invasion of France from England, was imminent. Even Hitler knew that. What none of us knew, including Hitler, were the date and place.

One day I flew down to the south coast where there was a Canadian Spitfire wing at Tangmere, Sussex. I talked to Lorne Cameron from Winnipeg, Commanding Officer of 401 Squadron, regarding a return to operational flying. He was most cooperative, and said that he would ask for me by name, and did so. I also went to H.Q. in London and signed a waiver of leave home in favour of returning to a squadron. It was, I thought, the wrong time to go back to Canada. I knew that I was short-cutting the system; I had only instructed for six weeks. But I was not busy and thought that I would be of more use back on ops.

On June 6, 1944, I was flying an old Hurricane down by the south coast when I saw the armada in the English Channel. The invasion of France was on! This was D-Day, and the Normandy beach was the place.

A few days later I reported to the Fighter Pilot Pool at Redhill, Surrey. I went up to Warwickshire for one day to see my brother, then down to

Tangmere on the coast where I joined 401 Squadron. I was back on ops after exactly six months.

401, 411 and 412 were RCAF Squadrons, and together comprised 126 wing. It would be a little different from an RAF Squadron in which Commonwealth pilots shared amazing esprit de corps, but should be fun. We were on the channel, facing France. I had some old friends in the wing and it was bound to be interesting. Things were happening quickly; under Squadron Leader Cameron, the boys had already shot down eight enemy aircraft over the beach-head, for the loss of just one Spitfire. This included Junkers 88s by Lorne Cameron (two), Jerry Billing, and Arthur Bishop. "Bish", the son of Air Marshal Billy Bishop of First World War fame, showed his father's touch in this scrap.

The next morning I was airborne early in a new Spitfire IX B. What an aircraft with a two-stage supercharger! We escorted Mitchells bombing the German coastal defence forces just south of the beach-head in Normandy. It was good to be in action again. As part of the Second Tactical Air Force, our job was close support to the Army. Therefore, we would go to France as soon as the beach-head could accommodate a landing strip.

Next day, we were airborne again, on a two-hour patrol over the beach. It was like old times: landing craft, tanks, guns, men, and the smoke of battle just as in Sicily and Salerno Beach. But this time it was on a grander scale with sixty miles of beach-head and the addition of two floating harbours called Mulberries, where vessels could dock. Five Allied divisions landed on the beaches, two American, two British, and one Canadian, to be met with fierce resistance by four German divisions. We remembered some old familiar names up at the top: Eisenhower as Commander in Chief, with Montgomery as Field Commander, opposite von Rundstedt as Commander In Chief, with Rommel as his Field Commander. But all that filtered down to us pilots was that Montgomery remembered how close the Allies had been to being pushed back into the sea at Salerno Beach. This time he was going to quickly establish a good base before Rommel could bring up reserves to turn us out.

And that was where the tactical support of the Spitfires came into play: we were a crucial element against the roads, railways and bridges in limiting the German build-up. The air power must hold the ring and clobber any movement of enemy reserves. The Germans, deliberately misled by many radio transmissions, had thought that the invasion would take place further east in the Pas de Calais. Even after the Normandy landing, Hitler thought that there would be another one at Calais, and held back armour. Rommel justifiably worried about our air power: would he be able to get his armour up to oppose the landing? Not that Spitfires would attack tanks; we did not. But rocket-equipped Typhoons and medium bombers attacked armour with a vengeance; and we were all part of Tactical Air Force. The fact was that it took Rommel three days to move a division from Brittany, only thirty miles, while the Allies could move a division across the channel in one day.

It was, therefore, not surprising that we were hedge-hopping most days in June, shooting up transport wherever we found it moving within a hundred miles of the front. We made it very difficult for the Wehrmacht to bring up supplies in daylight, and the days were at their longest in June.

On June 18, twelve days after the landing, the wing moved to a strip on the beach-head at Beny-sur-Mer, near Caen. We were in France. Now we could provide better service; we could be over the front two minutes after take-off.

From June 19th to 21st, a fluke gale hit the coast of Normandy. The two Mulberry harbours were damaged, ships were anchored, the war slowed to a crawl, and we couldn't fly. But on the 22nd we were airborne again, dive bombed a bridge in Cabourg, and lost a pilot to flak.

Throughout the rest of June we flew patrols, usually twice a day for each pilot, sometimes more, varying from protection of the army on the still narrow beach-head (Caen was only eight miles from the sea and had not yet been taken), to deep penetration and strafing of transport to the south and east. The situation was different from the relatively fixed front in the mountains north of Naples. In this open country, no transport movement whatever was allowed.

We did not see as many enemy aircraft as we had anticipated. Without doubt, the large Fortress formations of the U.S. Eighth Air Force, with their daily runs into Germany, kept many Focke-Wulfs and Me 109s for home defence. Goering also had to worry about the Russian front.

On June 28th we were about ten miles east of Domfront at 7,000 feet when we were jumped by a squadron of Focke-Wulf 190s out of the sun. A good old-fashioned scrap followed, right down to ground level. My new Spit IX was too much for a Focke-Wulf pilot who stayed around for the scrap. He had a good aircraft, but he could not turn with a Spit IX, and when I got on his tail I knew I had him. One short burst and he was into the trees in a great flash of fire. We got six Focke-Wulfs but lost two pilots, Scotty Murray and Bob Davidson.[1] Scotty had been a Flight Commander; when he failed to return they gave me his job at "A" Flight.

July 1st, Canada's birthday, was not a nice day at the beach-head. There was no flag waving; there was no time for nonsense. It was raining and the ceiling was down below 500 feet. It was the kind of day that the Huns might hit and run, and that was why we were patrolling the length of the beach, just below the cloud. The weather didn't bother me a bit; in fact, I rather enjoyed the challenge. The only problem was that the bridgehead was narrow in some places, and the rain and low clouds made it difficult to estimate exactly where the front was.

We had just turned around at the west end of our run, and Jerry Billing was on the south side of the section of four Spits over what was called No-man's land,

---

(1)
Scotty survived and eventually walked back; Bob was presumed killed.

that half-mile or so in between our troops and the German Army. The latter promptly let Jerry have it in the engine. He had no height to bale out.

He called me up at once. I spied a large green field out in front at eleven o'clock, a little toward our troops, and told Jerry to do a U-turn and put the Spit down on its belly in that field.

Jerry did it nicely, left a black streak across the field, jumped out and waved to us and ran like hell, his white silk scarf flying behind. I didn't see Jerry again until the war was over. It was the third time that he had been shot down, but he was never captured. I felt guilty about having brought him too close to the lines; it was my fault. But after Jerry's experience in Malta, I shouldn't have worried about him. He hid in the bullrushes, up to his neck in water, and the German soldiers couldn't find him. Then he had a pretty good time at a French farm for a month. The farmer just happened to have a daughter.

The next day we dive-bombed a bridge south of Caen, after which we flew deeper to the south looking for the Luftwaffe. We found about thirty aircraft flying east at about 11,000 feet, some 4,000 feet above us. We turned on the same course, and climbed toward these aircraft which, as we got closer, were obviously Me 109s. With their height advantage we were catching up in a steady climb which was just fine: we were in their blind spot when we overtook them.

I got behind a section of five 109s, and from 150 yards fired a burst at the nearest one. The 109 climbed east to 13,000 feet. I'm not sure why he did this; perhaps he didn't realize that my climb was superior. I got a couple more good squirts at him, and saw strikes on the fuselage. The Messerschmitt was obviously disabled. The prop was milling, and the pilot slowed to a glide. We were not too far south of Caen, and I thought it might be possible to get the pilot to glide north to our side of the front. Perhaps we could get a prisoner. I reluctantly closed the throttle and slowed down to 120 mph, and pulled in beside him, even though I felt somewhat uncomfortable at such a vulnerable speed. But we were alone; we appeared to have lost all the other aircraft, as was usually the case. I was on the right side of the 109, quite close with my left wing-tip about ten or twelve feet behind his right aileron. The 109 only had a number 6 on the fuselage, behind the black cross. The pilot wore a light tropical helmet, the kind we used in the Middle East; perhaps he had been out there. He looked at me, and I gestured with my arm, pointing back north unmistakably. He slowly banked the aircraft to the left and turned around to the north and straightened out, continuing to glide at 120 mph. He looked at me a number of times while I glided along beside him. I watched him carefully, but I was not afraid of his doing a kamikaze on me. I was sure that he was injured, probably in the legs. Otherwise, why wouldn't he bale out, or at least wave to me? But a lethargic turn of the head was all I could get out of him. Quite a few times I had been close to formation with 109s for a minute or so while lining one of them up, but never before had I got into tight formation with the enemy.

It became obvious that we were not going to glide as far as the front. As we got down near the ground, I opened the throttle and got my speed up, and circled around the 109, and watched until he made a rough but reasonable crash landing with landing gear up, in a field near Bernay. I took a quick run across the 109 on its belly with the camera gun. I did not see the pilot get out of the cockpit. I flew back to Beny-sur-Mer.

In this scrap, Bill Klersy, a very capable young pilot from Toronto, also got a 109.[2] We had no losses.

401 Squadron continued its heavy schedule of flying. There was no real problem except, perhaps, the flak and that came with the job. The fitters kept the engines serviced, the riggers patched the holes, and the armourers re-armed

(2)
Tragically, in May 1945, two weeks after the war had ended, Bill Klersy, DFC & Bar, C.O. of 401 Sqdn, was killed in a flying accident.

the 20 mm cannons and the machine guns. The pilots were all of good morale and ready to go.

Our friends flying Typhoons, superb heavier aircraft with 2400 horsepower, with their rockets slung under their wings, were the darlings of the army. The army directed them by radio contact with the pilot, to the German tanks and other armour. One could see them at any time of the day in shallow dives right over the front, firing the rockets at the Panzer armour. They were devastating. It was a dangerous job; the flak was even worse than we experienced. Our legacy was burnt-out transport lining the roads of Normandy. Nose-to-tail convoys a couple of miles long didn't have a single remaining vehicle. The Huns started putting flak-cars on the railroads and among the vehicles. It was impossible to strafe well-defended convoys without getting a few holes. Flak was not like enemy aircraft; skill could generally overcome the latter, while the avoidance of flak entailed a lot of luck.

On July 3rd we lost our C.O. while strafing in a hot spot near Alençon. His aircraft was hit in the engine, and Squadron Leader Cameron set it down on its belly pretty smartly. He was not captured by the Huns and lived with the Maquis for a month before moving to Bordeaux. He was turned over to the Gestapo by French collaborators, but en route to a prisoner of war camp he escaped and eventually was flown out of France, back to England.

In any case, 401 Squadron now needed a new C.O., and someone, perhaps George Keefer, our Wing Commander at the time, suggested me. And that was that. I was surprised, and felt inadequate for the job. But I had the signal in my hand, given to me by the Adjutant. At that moment we had to get airborne right away and there was neither the time nor anyone handy with whom to discuss the responsibility. I had often led the squadron in Italy and was not concerned about that aspect of the job; it was the administration with which I was unfamiliar. I needed a very competent adjutant, and knew a fellow named George Glover was available, so the next day I requested him and everything fell into place pretty quickly.

My job was to lead the squadron in the air and to co-ordinate it on the ground. With regard to operations, we received our daily direction from Wing H.Q., where the Wing Commander (Wingco Flying) supervised the flying activities of his three squadrons, and often flew with one of us. The C.O. of 126 Wing was Group Captain G.R. MacGregor, OBE, DFC, whose liaison (along with Wing Commander Keefer) with higher officers and the Army determined the nature of our daily flying. The exception to this was routine defensive readiness against enemy aircraft attack, which we continued throughout daylight hours.

When the Wing gave us our job, along with the relevant information, the Intelligence Officer would brief us with an up to date map, pointing out the position of our front-line troops, the enemy troops, armour or convoy, and anti-aircraft hot spots to avoid if possible. I would then advise the pilots who were flying on this sortie what we hoped to accomplish, the course, altitude, anticipated weather, and approximate course back to the beach-head if we got separated in a scrap. Routine patrols over the beach-head did not require briefing. Meanwhile the aircraft would have been re-armed and re-fuelled, with extra fuel tanks attached if necessary, supervised by Flight Sergeant White, the Senior N.C.O.

After the flight, the I.O. would meet us again to determine what we had accomplished. About once a week we met in the mess tent to review the cine-camera films from the aircraft which, with the pilot's name on the film, recorded his shooting ability or lack of it.

My ground duties were not onerous. Keeping up morale was not a problem: it might have been had the war been going badly. But we had to keep squadron discipline and strength, and there were letters to the next of kin. The Adjutant looked after the routine administration. The Engineering Officer with the Senior N.C.O. supervised the approximately one hundred ground-crew who kept our eighteen Spitfires serviceable. The Medical Officer was not as busy in his sick bay as the M.O.s had been, with malaria and hepatitis, in Sicily.[3]

It was an exciting time, the chief characteristic of which, I am sure, was how much activity was crammed into each long summer day. From 0400 hours to 2100 hours, the fighter squadrons were active. We often flew as twelve aircraft, a full squadron, when we were looking for enemy aircraft. But as time went on and we saw less of large enemy fighter formations, we frequently flew as four or eight aircraft sections. These were more flexible and manoeuvrable, especially for ground-strafing, and certainly for the narrow beach patrol. Routinely, "A" Flight, half the squadron, would be on duty from 1300 hours one day until 1300 hours the next, then have twenty-four hours off while "B" Flight took over. Every pilot flew two or three times daily, and we felt that it was only a matter of time until our armies would break out of this confinement and head for Paris, about a hundred miles away. But we weren't impatient. We knew that we had control over the bridgehead skies, and could roam freely a hundred miles behind. We had lots of time, a superb aircraft, an no shortage of pilots.

Not so the two armies locked in deadly struggle below. Rommel was alarmed when two of his S.S. Panzer divisions took eleven days to get from Germany to Normandy. Rommel himself was badly wounded when his staff car was shot up by a Spitfire. Hitler thought that the invasion had been brought under control, but von Rundstedt, his Commander in Chief, knew that he was facing twenty-five Allied divisions and could not contain them much longer. On July 5th, von Rundstedt advised Hitler to make peace. He was immediately relieved of his command, and succeeded by General Kluge.

Montgomery, who had hoped to capture Caen, only eight miles from the beach, on invasion day June 6th, still had not taken the city a month later. On July

---

(3)

See Appendix 5 for squadron strength.

7th, 750 Lancasters and Halifaxes of the RAF bombed Caen with 2,500 tons of bombs, virtually destroying William the Conqueror's ancient Norman capital of 1066. Our strip at Beny-sur-Mer was about five miles from Caen; we could feel the concussion of the bombing hit our chests. But we weren't on the ground long; I flew four times that day. Even this bombing did not allow the complete occupation of Caen by British and Canadians, and Churchill was impatient with Montgomery's lack of progress.

On July 9th, 442 Squadron joined our wing. We now had four Spit squadrons, and for the second time, Wing Commander Dal Russel took over 126 Wing. Dal was a true gentleman, whom the inelegance of war did not change. He was one of relatively few Canadians in the Battle of Britain in the first year of the war, and was now competently on his third tour of operations. His younger brother Hugh, also flying Spitfires, had been killed only three weeks earlier, yet he never mentioned it. I regret that I was not destined to have a long association with Dal, nor with his predecessor George Keefer. George, whom I got to like on very short acquaintance, also flew three tours of ops.

When 442 joined us at Beny-sur-Mer, two other characters that I knew from Malta days arrived. My old friend, Steve Randall from Toronto was a flight commander, and the irrepressible and irreverent Don Goodwin was attacking the enemy with gusto. Goodie had only recently been forced to bale out of his damaged Spitfire over the English Channel, and once again was rescued from the sea, this time by a Polish destroyer. Bill Olmsted was with 442, while Rod Smith of Regina, another experienced Malta veteran on our beach-head strip, was with 412 and later 401. It had been pure coincidence and not RAF policy when Rod arrived at Luqa, Malta, in 1942, and found his brother Jerry in the same squadron. They fought together in the blitz, helped each other out, and clobbered a goodly number of enemy aircraft. Eventually both were shot down into the sea; Rod alone was rescued.

It was one of the peculiarities of Fighter Command that the pilots with experience tended to survive, while the rookies made up most of the casualties. The reason was obvious; one learned the tricks. Not only did we become better pilots with experience, but learning to scan the sky to see the German aircraft before they attacked was essential. In consequence, the squadrons in Normandy were very strong with a high complement of veteran pilots. We were not at all worried about the Me 109s and Focke-Wulf 190s. We respected them as good fighters, and would like to have seen more of them.

But experience did not count nearly as much against the very effective German anti-aircraft flak. Flak, light under 8,000 feet and heavy shrapnel above that, was a daily greeting, and probably luck was as much a factor as skill in avoiding this fire from the ground. In spite of this, probably no army had ever received such a degree of close air support as our ground forces did from our Tactical Air Force. Rommel's expressed fear that Allied air superiority would interfere with the Wehrmacht's supplies proved to be entirely justified.

Somehow, I didn't see a lot of my old friends during July. Unlike Malta, we did not share a dispersal. They were on the other side of the strip, and we were airborne a lot of the time. I heard their voices in the air more than on the ground. When one flies several times a day, there's a tendency to sit down when the sun goes down. And the Huns bombed us every night at eleven sharp. They were so methodical and predictable, that it wasn't long until we began to crawl under the "three-tonner" trucks for protection at five to eleven. Some fellows dug slit trenches and put their camp cots in the trench with the tent over the top. This only protected against horizontal blast. The Junkers 88s would paste the strip at Beny for a few minutes, then leave.

Most of our losses, of course, occurred over enemy territory, and we didn't see the casualties. I only had cemetery duty once, when a pilot struggled back over the front and crashed. I attended the short service at the Beny cemetery, which was full of Canadian soldiers who had died on the beach-head. The bugler's "Last Post" was moving. I was inwardly relieved (and a little ashamed at that relief) that we never saw our casualties in the Air Force. I was glad to get into the Jeep with the Padre, and get back to the strip.

Throughout July we continued to provide constant air cover over the bridgehead, and extended our patrols 150 miles deep from Caen to Le Mans, Orléans, and Paris. This once again entailed the use of long-range fuel tanks. We lost a few pilots to flak while strafing, including the capable Bill Tew, but the squadron did well and got a dozen Focke-Wulfs and Me 109s. The elimination of German daylight transport remained our priority.

Montgomery, having failed to capture Caen on June 6th, used it as the focal point for successive blows against the German armour. The methodical Monty, as at El Alamein in North Africa, had trouble with the impatient, irrepressible Churchill, but he stuck to his scheme. On July 18th (when every pilot flew three times), RAF and USAAF carpet-bombed east of Caen, following which three British armoured divisions attacked the German Panzers. In very heavy fighting, our armour lost nearly two hundred tanks, but the havoc wreaked with the German armoured reserves, which had to be brought up to the battle at Caen, left the perimeter of the bridgehead weakened at Saint Lô.

British and Canadian casualties were heavy at Caen, but a week later, on July 25, when carpet-bombing shifted to Saint Lô, the Americans attacked with tenacity and suffered even greater losses while the German division defending Saint Lô almost ceased to exist. On July 26th the Panzer Lehr Armoured Division, which had been the strongest in the German army, had only fourteen tanks left out of two hundred.

Hitler ordered them to hold at all costs. This was impossible. They were forced to retreat. The line had been broken at Saint Lô. The Americans advanced three miles and the confinement of the bridgehead was over.

Although the fanatical Hitler still refused to acknowledge that the front was crumbling, and brought up more armour and ordered Field-Marshal von Kluge to counter-attack, this was, in fact, the beginning of the end.

And on that day, I was shot down.

Spitfire showing Normandy invasion stripes, painted on all allied aircraft at that time for identification by our troops. DND RE 20421

*Cameron, Halcrow, Husband, Cull, Klersy, Bell of 401 Squadron, RCAF,
just prior to Normandy invasion, 1944.*

Dick Cull, Bill Klersy and Gerry Bell.

137

*Wing Commander George Keefer, DSO,
DFC, from Prince Edward Island.
Flew three tours. DND PL 22165.*

*Wing commanderDal Russel, DSO, DFC,
from Montreal, flew from the Battle of
Britain to 1945. DND PL 22169.*

The author, C.O. 401 Squadron, Normandy, 1944.
DND PL 25867

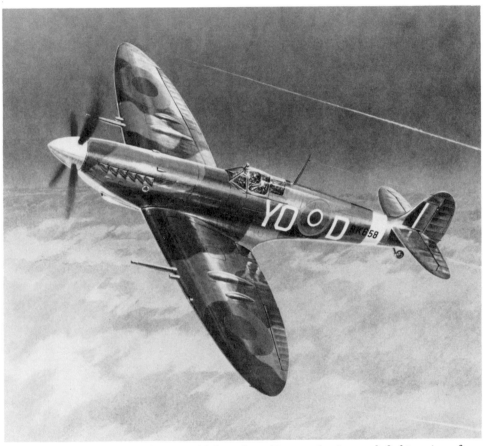

YO-D, the author's Spitfire IX, 401 Squadron, Normandy. A superb fighter aircraft.
Painting by R.W.Bradford, N.A.M.

Winston Churchill talks to us at Beny-sur-mer,
Normandy beach-head.

*Spitfire engine change, Normandy beach-head, 442 Squadron,
RCAF. DND PL 31363*

Chapter XII
"Le Paysan"

Mid July, 1944, Normandy. Field Marshal von Kluge, Commander-in-Chief German Forces in the West, to Adolf Hitler: "I arrived here with the firm intention of carrying out your orders to hold fast at all costs. But when one realizes that the price which must be paid consists of the slow but steady annihilation of our troops, then one cannot help entertaining the gravest doubts as to what the immediate future holds in store for this front... Despite all our fervent efforts, the moment is approaching when this sorely tried front will be broken. Once the enemy has penetrated into open country, organized operations will no longer be possible to control, owing to our troops' lack of mobility. As the responsible commander on this front, I regard it as my duty to draw your attention, my Fuehrer, to the consequences which will ensue.

At the commanders' conference south of Caen my closing words were: 'We shall hold fast, and if no help arrives in time to improve our position fundamentally, then we shall die an honourable death on the field of battle.'"

Flowers and Reeves in **The War 1939-1945**

July 26th, 1944, dawned a beautiful summer day with a fair westerly blowing the promise of day-long sunshine. It was the kind of day that French farmers got at their harvest. But the only harvest that the tacticians of the war were considering was a breakthrough after fifty-one days of confinement on the Normandy bridgehead.

Already the medium bombers from Second Tactical Air Force bases in England were winging it over our strip southwards toward the front at Saint Lô. It was their second day of blasting that particular point in the perimeter. We had been patrolling along the front lately from west of Saint Lô to the east of Caen, and only yesterday had escorted the Forts and Mitchells on the first carpet bombing of Saint Lô. The army called it "softening up" and after a modest advance yesterday, requested some accurate bombing today to ensure the breakout.

We had a different job this day. Our mechanics had slung thirty-gallon drop tanks on the Spits to give us an extra thirty minutes endurance. We were off on a deep sweep to Le Mans, Orléans and Paris, looking for enemy aircraft.

We got airborne from Beny-sur-Mer and climbed over the friendly beach to 8,000 feet, before turning south over the unfriendly front. The smoke rose from the fierce battle going on down below. Long gentle curves of red lights came lazily up toward our twelve Spitfires, the benign appearance of the tracers belying their lethal potential. But we were just beyond their range, moving along smartly and not concerned about light flak. We saw a half-dozen Typhoons playing follow the leader in long shallow dives, releasing their rockets at the German armour below, then pulling away to port or starboard amid the flak. Although the "Tiffies," as they were affectionately known, were diving at 400 mph, the released rockets' smoke trails left them far behind, and a few seconds later terminated in brilliant flashes on the ground. I'm sure that the Panzer commanders wondered where Goering's vaunted Luftwaffe was when the Typhoons attacked. But the Wehrmacht had had their day when their Stukas dive-bombed the Poles, French, and Russians. They had invented the "Blitzkrieg" and now it was coming home to roost. I looked down and didn't feel a bit sorry for them.

We flew due south for a hundred miles, then turned east around Le Mans over to Orléans, then north up to the Seine and Paris. The boys had their eyes open, but we didn't see any other aircraft except another squadron of Spits north of Dreux. It was a very pleasant trip — too pleasant in fact. We weren't out for a joy ride. Perhaps it was too nice a day; the Luftwaffe preferred a bit of cloud.

After lunch, whoever planned the sortie over at Wing H.Q. asked 401 Squadron to go around again. We were keen to take another run around by

Orléans and Paris. In the afternoon, as always, the warm air reflecting from the land cooled a few degrees at 1,500 feet to form a scattering strato-cumulus.

We had turned the corner south of Paris and were flying north-westerly near Dreux at 9,000 feet when heavy anti-aircraft guns suddenly let us have it. I was leading the twelve Spits.

There were only three bursts of heavy flak in quick succession, too quick for reaction: one explosion of steel shrapnel off the left wingtip, the second squarely in the engine just in front of my feet, the third off the right wingtip. The wounded aircraft shuddered with the violence of the shrapnel.

I knew that my Spitfire was badly hit. I lost power at once. I closed the throttle and looked at the temperature gauge; the needle ominously moved quickly to the right stop. The Spitfire was finished; I would have to get out quickly. Rather objectively, I reflected that it had been very good shooting to pick me off. I was out in front, only three bursts of flak, no time to move out of it.

"Get out boss, you're on fire!" It was Blue One or Yellow One, I don't know which, who woke me to action. Flying along-side, they could see the fire coming back from the engine toward the cockpit. There was no time for the formality of a call-sign; the informal greeting was very much to the point.

"Barley Blue One. Red One here," I answered. "Take over. I'm O.K. Course home is three hundred degrees. See you guys later. Cheerio."
"Get out now. The fire's spreading!" someone yelled.

I had slowed to a glide at 120 mph. I trimmed the aircraft to fly hands off, no problem. Smoke was coming back when I pulled the canopy jettison; nothing happened. So I slid it open the way we always did before landing, and opened the door on my left, took off my helmet, and undid my harness. I checked my parachute ring, stood up, and jumped easily out through the door.

I delayed pulling the rip cord for a few moments. I thought that it might be advantageous to get down quickly. I had no concern about the 'chute. There was only the noise of the wind. Then I pulled it. My momentum stopped with a rude jerk, the parachute billowed overhead, and I was suspended in the blue sky. It was perfectly still. I looked at my watch; it was twenty minutes past four.

I still had about six thousand feet to go. This would be very pleasant if the Huns weren't waiting for me on the ground. I did not want to spend the rest of the war in a prison camp. The immediate objective was to avoid capture; that might be difficult on such a beautiful afternoon. I looked down at the patchwork below, green pastures, woods and yellow ripening grain. I noticed that there was quite a strong west wind blowing me easterly across the dusty country roads.

Then I saw the cause of the dust. I was now about 2,000 feet up; below me was an open car with several men in it, driving north on a concession road. The car stopped. The wind carried me over it. The car took off at speed, turned right at the next road, moved a mile east, then right again on the next concession road. I drifted over them again. The open car moved another mile to the east and stopped again in my line of drift. For the third time, the strong west wind blew me over the car. This time I was quite low and could plainly see the four German soldiers in the open staff car. The wind was frustrating the soldiers; it might save me, with a bit of luck.

I hit the ground and rolled over unhurt beside a sandy road, probably a farm lane. A house was nearby. I jettisoned the 'chute quickly. A large French woman who had watched me coming down was at my side immediately. She gathered up my 'chute and stuffed the yards of silk up under her dress.

"Où sont les Allemands?" I blurted out in high school French.

"Là-bas!" She pointed to the road at the end of the lane. "Ils viennent. Cours! Vite! Vite!"

I knew what she was saying, and her actions left no doubt that the Huns were coming down the road. She was on my side.

There was a small barn about a hundred feet to the east. I ran to it, started to get in through a window, then changed my mind. It was too obvious. I laid my flying gloves on a beam inside the window, I'm not sure why except that they were of no more use to me, and took off at full speed for a small woods about a hundred yards away. As I took a dive into the woods, I heard the car roaring up the lane toward the French woman. They shouted at her. She delayed them for a vital moment. They took the parachute from her.

I got up and ran quickly through the woods, trying not to break any noisy branches. Another hundred yards and I was through. I thought that they would inevitably look for me in the woods. Best not to stop there. East of the woods I found a large ten-acre field of grain with a dirt farm road dividing it down the middle. The wheat was ripe, an excellent crop of golden grain up to my chest in depth.

This was it, I decided. I had time, I thought, for eight or ten full-speed leaps and bounds into the wheat in the left half, trying not to knock down a tell-tale path. Then I got down on my hands and knees and crawled a couple of hundred yards more, keeping my direction by the sun. I collapsed on my belly.

Presently the army car came around the left end of the woods, and proceeded down the dirt road that divided the wheat field. I heard it stop opposite me. I could faintly hear the soldiers talking. They commenced firing their rifles. Bullets were whistling overhead. There is something very unnerving about the whistle of bullets, much more than the bang, bang of firing. The immediate reaction is certainly to stand up with the hands overhead, which I very nearly did.

Then I thought that I should sneak a look at these guys. I lifted up slowly. I was glad that my hair was fair, about the colour of the grain, I thought. The four soldiers were standing in the open car, two in front, two behind, firing their rifles randomly in the air. Occasionally one would lower the barrel to fire over the wheat. They had no idea where I was! I lay down again quickly. I was laughing.

"You bastards!" I said. "You almost got me. I must remember to tell Intelligence about this trick when I get back."

I felt fine. I lay on my back and ate the kernels of ripe wheat. I had won the first round. I would stay here until dark, about four and a half hours away.

About seven o'clock, the soldiers had had enough of this game. They knew that I was there somewhere, but weren't prepared to tramp the whole field. They were tired and hungry. I watched them take off in the car.

Shortly after, lying in the grain, I was aware of footsteps and chatter. I did not move. Surely they would go by. But three small French boys stumbled and fell over me. They were startled, but recovered quickly. They, too, were looking for me, and as is often the case, knew better than the adults how to find me. They had brought me a tin full of sweet cherries, and the heel of a loaf of bread. I was hungry and ate it all. They told me to stay there while they got me some clothes, and left.

In an hour I watched them return. I wasn't sure how much I could trust them, so I had moved. But they were alone, and had the clothes, which I put on. They were pretty ragged; a shirt, pants that were six inches too short, and an old suit coat. But I happily traded my blue battle dress for them. Two boys each got a brass Canada pin from the shoulders of the battle dress. I compensated the third with the few coins I had. The kids left well satisfied with their adventure, as was I.

After nine o'clock it was getting dark, and I thought it was time to move. We knew through Intelligence the habits of the Germans. They would look intensively for three days for pilots or other aircrew, after which the search was called off. They could not afford more time than that. After three days, one only got caught on a routine check of identity card. I, therefore, had to be very careful for three days, even if it meant going hungry. I decided to head for a large mature woods I could see about a mile away.

Walking south down a dirt road in the dusk, I suddenly saw a man approaching me on foot. It was too late to turn. It was a German soldier, but he wasn't any bigger than I was. It was the first test of my ragged coat and high-water pants. He glanced at me and went by; not a word. Maybe he had a girlfriend. I continued on to the woods, got under a big beech tree where there were a lot of leaves, made a good bed, and pulled a foot of leaves over me just as it started to rain. Good, I thought, the rain would destroy any scent; they might bring dogs the next day. I was cozy and dry, and fell asleep.

The next day I continued to lie low. I heard dogs, but was not sure whether they were looking for me or if it were merely coincidental. I watched a nearby farmhouse from the edge of the woods. There were two young men, a girl, and an older couple. The old fellow had a limp. There were no soldiers around. By evening I thought it safe to approach, and knocked on the door. They appeared surprised to see a stranger, but I felt at once that I could take a chance with them. They were seated around a big kitchen table. I entered quickly, and looking at the older couple said, "Bonsoir Madame et Monsieur. Je suis le pilote qui est tombé hier. Je suis Canadien."

The reaction was spontaneous and friendly. They had seen the Spitfire go down. They were all talking at once. I couldn't follow it at all, but it didn't matter. Another place was set at the table, and only after a good meal did they tell me how dangerous it was. The kitchen door was locked. The countryside was full of German soldiers who had already offered a reward for me in the nearby town. They had given my parachute to the mayor as a gesture of goodwill. Regretfully, these people could not keep me there. I understood that readily enough, and thanked them kindly for the supper. I shook hands with every one in turn, listened to the old guy talk about the Boches from the First War, in which he had lost his leg, and went back to the woods. At least my belly was full, and I had seen fruit and vegetables from their garden for future reference.

The next day in the woods I saw two men in civilian clothes, approaching across a clearing. I might have avoided them, but they appeared to be looking for me, were slightly built, did not look at all military, so I did not hide. They spoke French, wanted to know my name, rank and number, what aircraft I flew, my squadron, and place and date of birth.

I didn't know who they were. I gave them my name, rank and number, which was all I was obliged to do under international law. They got pretty crusty. I told them to go to hell, and they left. But I understood that they would be back.

The next day, one of them returned with another fellow who could speak English. He told me that they must have the requested information to prove my identity. The Germans were planting imposters to trap them.

I decided to trust them. The Germans knew what I was flying anyway, because what was left of the Spitfire was just a couple of miles away. I gave them my squadron, aircraft, birth date and place.

I moved a couple of hundred yards and watched them return the following day from my new location. Too many of our fellows had been turned in for generous German bribes. But they were alone. I spoke to them, and the fellow who spoke fairly good English said, "You are O.K. We have been in touch with England. They have confirmed your birth date and place, and that the Commanding Officer of 401 Squadron was lost on July 26th. We are Maquis. We will help you. We will arrange to fly you back to England by Lysander some night very soon."

How they got away with these radio messages to England year after year, right under the Germans' noses, was beyond me. But they did it, and most of the time got away with it. Some were caught and executed.

They also told me that they had arranged with the old farmer's wife and daughter, Madame and Simone Esprit, that I could stay up in the small hayloft in the barn for a few days, and they would bring me food. But I must not have any contact at all with the men. They knew nothing of this; the fewer involved, the better.

I had heard about the French underground Maquis and the Lysanders flying downed aircrew, spies, and VIPs from small fields in France at night, across the channel to England. It was among the most dangerous and fascinating deeds of intrigue in the war. It was also the quickest way home. I knew a couple of fellows who had been picked up by a "Lizzie" at night, but they were sworn to secrecy. The alternative route back to Britain was over the Pyrenees to Spain and Gibraltar, a long dangerous trip. I was all for having a crack at the Lysander.

A couple of days later, I met the Maquis again in the woods. Regretfully they informed me that with the break-through at Saint Lô, the Lysander programme had become too dangerous; there were too many German soldiers about. The plans had changed: they would get me a passport and let me walk back. They had a camera, and with a white sheet behind my head, took my photograph right there in the woods. One of them would go to Rouen, about sixty miles, on a bike, to get me a Belgian identity card.

I was impatient to get going, but I knew that they were risking their lives to help me, and I respected their judgement. Anyone caught helping Allied airmen to escape, and there were many, was immediately shot by the Gestapo.

The hayloft was hot and dry on August afternoons. I was thirsty, left the barn, and climbed over the high stone wall around the garden behind the barn. I was eating red currants when a German soldier came in through the only garden gate. I took a dive under the currant bushes; I did not want a confrontation without a passport.

The bushes were old and fortunately very heavy. The soldier walked down the row next to the one in which I was lying on my stomach, with my face in the sandy loam. He stopped. His army boots were not more than twenty-four inches from by nose. I wondered if he were looking toward the end of the garden, or at my back. Did he have a gun? Should I grab his ankles and upset him? I remained still.

He did not see me. The boots turned around in front of my face, and walked away. I heard the gate shut. I went over the wall and back up to the loft.

A few days later I heard an unmistakable dogfight going on overhead. I recognized the Merlins and the whistle of Spitfires, and was down the ladder and out into the barnyard in a jiffy. I saw the Spits overhead, one firing at an Me 109. They came down low, and I got a close look at them. I could hardly believe it! There was a YO on the Spit; it was my own 401 Squadron.

Some empty 20 mm shells fell from the cannons of the Spit into the barnyard. By God, that was good! My immediate reaction was that I had to get back to the squadron. What excitement! What stimulation! In the ecstasy of the moment I forgot where I was, and I almost didn't care. Fortunately, I was already re-entering the barn when some German soldiers came into the yard to get a drink. They came straight to the cider barrels.

(I wouldn't touch the cider because I had watched the men adding water to the barrels from the small pond in the barnyard. The cattle drank the stagnant water that drained the yard, but I wouldn't. Perhaps the bacteria helped ferment the cider!)

I had no time to climb the ladder to the loft behind the barrels. I took a dive onto the hay behind the old cider press, and feigned sleep. I was in plain view if they looked behind the press while they took cider from the barrels. They left me undisturbed. Later Simone brought me two of the empty 20 mm cannon shells from the barnyard.

It was two weeks before the Maquis returned from Rouen with my passport. During that time it was hot and dry in the hayloft, and I had lots of time to think. I thought of swimming in cool water, and eating ice cream. But these were not important. I read the only English book on the farm, "My Man Jeeves" by P.G. Wodehouse, a gem of a paperback. But I was impatient to get going. I was always impatient to get to the next job, but this was different.

I knew that my younger brother was due to go on ops about this time, and while Bomber Command was different from Fighter Command, it was still Air Force, and the basic rules of flying applied. What I wanted to do, what came back to me again and again, was to go to England as soon as possible, and see these fellows, all of the crew, and tell them how to survive. That was it, in a nutshell. There was a very small margin, when flying operationally, between surviving and dying. I did not want to dramatize it, and I acknowledged that luck played a great part in one's destiny. Nevertheless, the pilots and aircrew who did not make mistakes, who knew the "tricks" (which essentially were the pursuit of good habits and the avoidance of errors) were the ones who survived. And I wanted to emphasize these few simple rules of good flying to each crew member so that he would not let the others down.

This, then, was the basis of my impatience to get out of occupied France.

Finally, word came to meet the Maquis in the woods. They handed me my passport with attached photo. Henceforth, I would be Jacques Michel Kattchix, a Belgian farm labourer. I thanked the two fellows and shook hands. Simone and her mother gave me an old hoe to put over my shoulder. My clothes were scruffy and I certainly looked the part: "un paysan". My French was poor, but possibly as good as the average German soldier whom I might encounter. I was ready to have a crack at it. I thanked Madame Esprit and Simone for all the meals they had carried out to me in the barn, said "au revoir" and walked away westerly.

I did not know how far I would have to go to find friendly territory. I had been shot down eighty miles behind the lines, but the breakthrough at Saint Lô had taken place, and perhaps the Allied armies were half-way to me. The prudent thing to do to avoid becoming a Prisoner of War, was to shun a confrontation with German troops. Therefore, I would have to curb my impatience, avoid towns and main roads, and stick to my identity in behaviour while making my way westerly along back roads.

I had taken a few precautions in the hayloft. While washing my shorts and socks (the rest of my clothes were French), I had removed all labels. I had cut the tongues out of my shoes where there was a "Made in England" tag. I had no money; I had given Mme. Esprit what I had, sixty-five dollars worth of new Allied Forces French francs. I had a French pipe, a bruyère that the boys had bought me in Bayeux, a tobacco pouch (empty), and my passport. If necessary, I could survive a search.

My journey went pretty well, athough I didn't get very far the next couple of days. There was very little traffic on the dirt roads; at night, I could hear some trucks a mile or so to the north. I met a troop of German soldiers walking east; they hardly looked at me, and appeared listless. No doubt they were relieved to be getting away from the front, even though they had no transport.

That night when I was in a wood, I heard the guns. For a moment I doubted it, then I knew quite definitely that it was heavy artillery. Sound carries better at night, and the prevailing westerly brought the booming to me. It meant that the artillery was only about fifteen miles away. The front was getting closer. It would not be long now. I had a good sleep.

The next day there were greatly increased numbers of German soldiers on the road, too many for comfort. I took to the fields, but walking was not as good. I was poking along near the edge of a grain field when I heard aircraft coming from the west. Two Thunderbolts were flying along at about two thousand feet. Several Me 109s came down on them from behind. I knew what was coming and yelled at them to "Break around!" Futile, to say the least. One of the Thunderbolt pilots baled out right overhead. I watched the parachute for a moment but realized that it would draw German soldiers by the dozen. I moved smartly out of the field back to the road, while some soldiers ran by me to surround the parachute. I don't know what happened to the other Thunderbolt but there was too much traffic on the road (not vehicles, but soldiers), and I was tempting fate. So I moved off the road again into a wood of big mature trees. I sat down, feeling sorry for the Thunderbolt pilots.

Thunderbolts were designed for, and were good at strategic escort above 25,000 feet. Their performance at low-level tactical support was completely inadequate.

That evening I heard machine guns rattling, and knew that the front was not far away. I would go no further, I was in a good spot, and would let the fighting go over the top of me. I could hear armour a mile away to the north, but did not think that they would deliberately choose to go through this mature forest. At least it seemed illogical, although I did not know their habits. I could hear some shells whistling overhead: it was difficult to be sure of their direction.

Before sunset, the machine gun fire changed to sporadic cracks of rifle fire. I found it interesting and thought "This is the way it should evolve; this should be the last phase." I was excited with the experience. I was in a good spot; these big trees offered more protection than a barn that they might lob a few shells at. All the roads were busy. I slept hardly at all that night, and didn't care. I propped my back against a big tree, and listened to the sounds, including soldiers walking by on the road, and watched a few tracers' lights whistling overhead.

About seven-thirty the next morning, I heard a vehicle coming along the road from the west. I moved carefully to the edge of the wood to see it. It stopped not too far from me. It was a Jeep, with two American soldiers. I was not about to let it get away, and walked quickly toward them. I still had my hoe. They watched me carefully, the Jeep motor running. Neither of them moved.

I said "Good-day fellows, It's nice to see you guys."
"Jeez, you speak good English," the one on the right said.
"I should," I replied, "I'm a Canadian."
"What are you doin' here?" he asked.
"I was shot down a month ago," I answered.
"This is no place to talk," the driver, a sergeant, interrupted.
"Just below that grade there are several pockets of German troops."

He pointed to the south, about three hundred yards away, down to the bottom of a field.

"They're watching us right now," he said. "We'll have to take them out shortly. We'll take you back a mile or two. The Intelligence Officer will want to see you."

"That suits me fine," I replied, climbing into the back of the Jeep. "Do you mind if I bring my hoe?"

There was a faint smile as he wheeled the Jeep around, and we were off.

The author as Jacques Michel Kattchix in occupied France, 1944.

Chapter XIII
The Yorkshireman

(Ref. Map: Normandy 2)

No man is an Iland, intire of itselfe; every man is a peece of the Continent, a part of the maine; if a Clod bee washed away by the Sea, Europe is the lesse, as well as if a Promontorie were, as well as if a Mannor of thy friends, or of thine owne were; Any Mans death diminishes me, because I am involved in Mankinde; And therefore never send to know for whom the bell tolls; It tolls for thee.

John Donne in "Devotions," 1624

The two Americans took me back a few miles in the Jeep to a field where soldiers were busily erecting several marquees. The Sergeant turned me over to his Lieutenant who in turn called in the Intelligence Officer. The I.O. got a signal away to 83 Group RAF, to which our wing belonged, and in a little while got things straightened out a bit. At least they confirmed who I was, and I was then able to go to the mess tent and get something to eat. It was the first American rations I had had since I had been in Italy, and the food was as welcome and pleasing as the weiners had been on Salerno Beach about a year earlier.

The I.O. informed me that I would have to go to an Interrogation Centre and make an official report on my experience in occupied territory. The camp was back near Caen; he wasn't sure exactly where it was, but would find out. It was fenced in and no one was allowed to leave until he had been interrogated. It happened that he was going back to Argentan and Falaise shortly and I could get a ride at least that far with him. He might be obliged to take me all the way: he could not turn me loose. That suited me fine; I knew Falaise from the air and it was not far from Caen. The sooner I got there, the better.

We hadn't gone very far and were driving down a pleasant tree-lined main street in a town when he stopped the Jeep beside an outdoor café. The town had just been liberated the previous day, and was still in a state of mixed jubilation and fear, in spite of which the cafés were functioning. People were laughing and chatting, and sipping wine in the shade of the canopies. I felt an unfamiliar sense of pleasant relaxation.

Then a noisy commotion began nearby with people shouting and women screaming. A crowd chased a young woman who ran past our Jeep, her face panic-stricken. She was cornered and I jumped out and ran over to find out what was going on. I was assured that they were not going to hurt her. They held her roughly and firmly while a woman produced a scissors and cut all of her hair off tight to the scalp. It was the standard treatment for fraternizing with German soldiers, they told me. When the job was done, they turned her loose and jeered derisively while she ran away.

It was the day following the German army retreat from this part of Normandy toward the Seine. I was completely unprepared for the carnage that we encountered on the road, in the ditches, and in the fields along the roadside. We crawled along in the summer heat toward Argentan. Frequently, we had to stop where there was only single lane traffic due to burnt-out armoured cars, artillery vehicles, tanks, and trucks clogging the road. But in many places we were stopped, and finally turned around by burial parties trying to gather up and identify the twisted and shattered remains of German soldiers lying along the road. Until then, I had not known that the German army still heavily depended upon horses for mobility; hundreds of dead horses impeded our progress. We finally tried another road to Falaise.

Lacking all news for four weeks, I had not been aware of the terrible battle that had taken place until this day, August 22nd. The success of the allied breakout from the Normandy bridgehead, of which this battle was the climax, was really the beginning of the end of this war. The defeat of the German

Seventh Army has been called the greatest disaster in modern military history.[1]

Hitler's obdurate fanaticism in Normandy cost more German than Allied lives. It had started in late June following the prolonged heavy losses of armour around Caen. Field Marshals Rommel and von Rundstedt returned to Germany and asked Hitler for a reappraisal of tactics: the senseless attrition of armour could not continue. They were treated contemptuously, lectured and dismissed. Back in Normandy, Rundstedt telephoned Field Marshal Keitel in Berlin. When Keitel asked him what he thought they should do, Rundstedt replied, "End the war, you fools!"[2] Rundstedt, as recorded earlier, was immediately relieved of his command, to be succeeded by Field Marshal von Kluge on July 6th.

The next episode occurred July 20th, when a group of disillusioned army officers attempted to assassinate Hitler. Colonel von Stauffenberg placed a bomb under a conference table at Hitler's Headquarters. The plan miscarried;

---

(1)

> *The defeat of the German Sixth Army at Stalingrad in 1943 was a close second. There Hitler had absolutely refused General Paulus permission to withdraw or even to attempt a breakout after being surrounded by superior forces.*
>
> *"Hoping for a gesture of honourable defiance, Hitler promoted Paulus to field marshal's rank by signal on 30 January. No German field marshal had ever surrendered to the enemy and he thus 'pressed a suicide pistol into Paulus's hand'. At this final imposition of authority Paulus baulked. On 30 January his headquarters were overrun and he surrendered with his staff to the enemy. The last survivors capitulated on 2 February, leaving 90,000 unwounded and 20,000 wounded soldiers in Russian hands. 'There will be no more field marshals in this war', [an angry] Hitler announced . . . 'Here's a man who has 45,000 to 60,000 of his soldiers die defending themselves bravely to the end – how can he give himself up to the Bolsheviks?'"*
>
> *John Keegan in **The Second World War***

(2)

> *Flower and Reeves, **The War 1939 - 1945***

Hitler was only slightly wounded. Several conspirators, including von Stauffenberg, were shot that same evening.

Even though Rommel was seriously injured and in hospital at that time, Hitler suspected him and Kluge of complicity in the bomb plot. In October, Rommel would be forced by Generals loyal to Hitler to commit suicide because of his suspected involvement in this plot. In July, Hitler decided that the test of Kluge's loyalty to him would be a successful counter-attack with all available armour into the flank of the American spearhead that was driving rapidly southwards from Saint Lô. Fourteen hundred German tanks were to drive west from Mortain to the sea. (See map Normandy 2)

But the Canadian and Polish Armoured Divisions had driven south from Caen to Falaise, and the U.S. Third Army had advanced rapidly far to the south and east, to Le Mans, then hooked north up to Argentan. Field Marshal Kluge knew that his half-million men, counter-attacking westwards against impossible odds, were going the wrong way into an enormous trap. But he could do nothing about Hitler's order.

His first attack on August 7th failed. On August 10th, Hitler ordered Kluge to attack further south-west, precisely the manoeuvre for self-destruction. On August 15th, Hitler, unable to contact Kluge whose staff-car, like Rommel's earlier, had been strafed by aircraft, fired his Field Marshal and ordered him back to Germany. Kluge took his dismissal quite calmly, and that night wrote a letter to Hitler imploring him to end the unequal battle in the West. But Kluge knew that he would be met in Germany by the Gestapo, and on the way home the next day took poison.

Too late, Hitler changed his mind. The German Army turned around, and the Hitler Youth Division held open the neck of the Falaise pocket until August 21st, allowing 300,000 soldiers to escape to the east. But they left behind 200,000 prisoners and 50,000 dead. By the morning of August 22nd, the fighting had virtually ceased, leaving behind the carnage that now surrounded me.

I had never expected to see this ugly side of the war. Only by accident did I arrive at the Falaise Gap on this day . . . the day after the gap was closed, the fighting just ended. We could hear the distant guns away off to the east where the few Panzer remnants of the German Seventh Army were retreating, hounded, toward the Seine. But everything was quiet here.

This road was blocked too; there had been no escape here. We would have to make a long detour. All at once it seemed vulgar to attempt to go anywhere in a hurry.

"Would you hold it a minute, Captain?" I asked.

The Intelligence Officer switched off the Jeep, and there was only silence. Not a sound. Not even the birds had yet recovered. There were no aircraft overhead. The scene of battle had shifted far to the east already; only the dead remained. The ripe, yellow unharvested grain wafted gently in the soft breeze as though it were a consoling blanket over the bodies of horses and men. But the undulating blanket of the grain field could not hide the grotesquely protruding wide-angled legs of horses in rigor mortis. Nor did it cover the bodies of the soldiers who lay as they had fallen by the roadside. In the heat of the August afternoon the awful smell of death assailed our nostrils.

"Man's inhumanity to man makes countless thousands mourn," I said absently.
"Who said that? What has happened to humanity?" asked the I.O.
"Oh God, I don't know," I thought to myself, unexpectedly tired with the seeming overwhelming futility of it all. Then, of course, it all came back to me. It was years earlier: Malcolm MacEachern, quoting Robert Burns to my parents in our old brick home in the village near Ottawa, would discuss "that ill opinion which makes thee startle at me, thy poor earth-born companion, and fellow mortal." And Mother responded with that most beautiful Burns song, "My Luve is like a Red, Red Rose".

I had gone to the MacEachern farm, a half-mile away, with my friend Keith after school, and saw Mac thumbing through his ancient, worn copy of Burns, carefully picking up and placing in their proper order the loose pages that had fallen on the well-scrubbed white pine kitchen floor. I picked up a page and handed it to him. He glanced at it and said: "Aye. 'That man to man, the world o'er, shall brithers be for a' that.'" I think it was his favourite.

Then war came, and nine months later when school got out in 1940, Keith and I, now eighteen and impatient to get at it, enlisted in the Royal Canadian Air Force.

We matured in a hurry; more gradually, and long before Keith was shot down[3] we knew what this war was all about. We learned that democratic peoples, reluctant to get involved in war, are slow to recognize fiends; dictators are always fast off the mark.

This war was not a political accident. It was very deliberately planned by a man with a twisted mind who had acquired enormous dictatorial powers, a fiendish man who believed in the superiority of one race over another, who believed that it was legitimate for these racially "superior" specimens to systematically exterminate the "lesser" people.

And now, five years after Hitler's Army had overwhelmed Poland, it was paying the ultimate price here. The Allies' aim in Normandy was to destroy the German Seventh Army where it stood, and not to chase their armour half-way across Europe. When Hitler refused to permit von Kluge to withdraw, he invited the catastrophe of Falaise exactly as he had done eighteen months earlier at Stalingrad.

My companion had felt this tragedy too, and had indulged my silence. Now he re-phrased his question about man's inhumanity to man, and asked "Where has humanity gone?" And now I could answer him.

---

(3)
Keith MacEachern's Lancaster bomber was shot down over Germany in 1943. He survived the infamous long march by the Baltic Sea in mid-winter 1945, during which some prisoners of war died. When he was liberated at war's end, Keith weighed barely 100 pounds; his black hair was pure white. He was 23.

"Before the war, Captain, I heard an old family friend quote Robert Burns quite often," I replied. "But I'm sure that humanity is not permanently dispossessed. It is only suspended, temporarily, while an ugly war is fought against a tyrant. There is no other way. There can be no compromise."

We left this terrible place, by-passed Falaise and the ruins of Caen, and eventually got to the Interrogation Centre. It was a common camp for American and Commonwealth Air Force aircrew. There were more than sixty pilots awaiting extensive questioning by Intelligence Officers. Primarily, this was with regard to names and locations of French citizens who had helped us evade capture and acquire French identity cards. Of course, we had not asked and generally did not know the names of our friends in the Maquis.

But there were many other intelligence concerns, and we were detained four days. We were given temporary identity cards, travel vouchers, and a little money. I wanted to get back to England and tried, to no avail, to hurry up the process.

While there, I learned that my former squadron had moved a few miles south from the bridgehead to another strip. I went back to the squadron and received an enthusiastic greeting. Not unexpectedly, there were quite a few new faces; a month is a long time in a war. I learned that my successor, Charlie Trainor of Charlottetown, Prince Edward Island, had been shot down. Consequently, there was a vacancy again for a C.O. at 401 Squadron. (Charlie and my old friend, Steve Randall, ended up as prisoners of war.) The Adjutant told me that on the day I was shot down, I had been awarded a Bar to the D.F.C.

That afternoon, five of us raggedly-looking chaps from the wing were flown from B-14 airfield to London.[4] We got some clean underclothing, booked into the old Regent Palace Hotel, and luxuriated in warm baths. We

(4)

See Appendix 6

had to tolerate our untidy clothes for one more day, however, and were politely asked for identification several times by London bobbies.

The next day, we all went to RCAF HQ. I wanted to see someone in Personnel about the vacancy back at 401 Squadron, and was surprised when a staff officer said that Air Marshal Breadner would see me. But apparently this was his custom. I still had the "paysan" clothes on when shown into his posh office. I had not met the Air Marshal previously, and found him kind and not at all impersonal. I was touched by his remark that when we were shot down there were a few tears among the office girls who closely followed our exploits. But I thought he might be exaggerating, or "laying it on a bit," as they called it in England. The important thing was that he promised to consider my request to return to 401 Squadron. But first, I had to get two weeks leave and pay, and then my uniform and the rest of my kit out of warehouse storage in London. I would also require new battledress, gloves, and a helmet equipped with oxygen mask, radio R/T and goggles. I would be ready to fly again.

Headquarters advised me that my brother, Carleton, was at an Operational Training Unit in Yorkshire, the last stage of training before posting to a squadron. On September 2nd, all my chores in London being completed, I took the train northward for Yorkshire. I got to the O.T.U. in the evening, but found that Tot and his crew (for some reason a different and younger crew than I had met in Bournemouth) had been posted to 434 Squadron at Croft, not far away.

There was good bus service; I got over to Croft just before midnight. I could see the great, black, hulking outlines of the Halifax III four-engined bombers on the airport. I went to the Officers' Mess and found a half-dozen aircrew having a snack.

"Excuse me, fellows," I said. "Would any of you be able to tell me where I might find my brother, Flying Officer Kennedy?"
One fellow said "Wasn't he with Todhunter's crew?"

"Yes, I believe so," I answered.

"I'm sorry, old chap," he replied, "but we buried the whole crew today."

"Are you sure? Is there a possibility that my brother wasn't flying with the crew, sick or something?" I asked, knowing it was a futile hope.

"No, I'm sure he went in with them. All seven were killed. It was their first trip on Ops. I'll get the Padre and he'll tell you about it."

He went to fetch the Padre. I sat down in the lounge. I felt completely devastated. I saw the copies of "Flight" and "Aeroplane" on the coffee table in front of the fireplace, as they were in all of the RAF Officers' Messes in England. Soon my brother's name would be listed among the casualties in the back pages, I thought abstractedly.

The Padre had a list of the boys who had died August 30th. Tot's name was there.

It was their first operational sortie. The Padre had buried the seven over at Harrogate that morning. He knew nothing of the cause of the crash. He kindly arranged to put me up for the night, and I thanked him for coming out to see me.

I put on my cap and trench coat and went out for a walk. For the first time in the war I was really hurt. I was overwhelmed by the sudden absolute finality of it all. I was glad that it was raining softly because the rain would hide a grown man's tears.

Getting shot down myself had not been a problem. I had treated the whole thing as an adventure. I played a game with the German soldiers. But this was completely different. This was not fair. These young lads didn't have a chance; they were killed before they learned a thing about survival.

I walked out through the gates past the guard, and down the road in the rain, and as I walked, I cursed Hitler, the mad fanatic who said that he was going to conquer the world. No matter the cost. Millions of lives. Millions of mothers crying when they learned their sons were lost. The Germans themselves lost more than any country except the Soviet Republics. All for this God damned mad man's ambitions. I had felt relatively invulnerable, although I knew I wasn't, but finally he had got to me. He had done it after all. God damn Hitler and damn the whole war and everything associated with it.

I thought of my mother. My parents would know by now. Dad, an old soldier badly wounded on the Somme in the First World War, would not say much. Long before, in Flanders Fields, he had seen the rows of crosses. Mother would derive a great deal of comfort from her faith. It was appropriate that she should. Walking in the rain I was grateful for that. I was quite conscious of the fact that I had no such faith myself from which to seek solace. I thought that a spiritual existence in another life was a beautiful concept. It was hope when there was no hope. I wished that it were true for Tot's sake. But in the rain that night in Yorkshire, it was an ancient myth that I could not resolve. I only knew that my brother's life was over, abruptly terminated at twenty-one years. And I was angry that fate should have been so unkind.

Next morning I spoke to the Commanding Officer of Tot's Squadron. He told me that the crew had returned from Germany and were circling the airport at 1,500 feet awaiting permission to land, when the aircraft quite suddenly dove into the ground. All seven boys were killed instantly. The cause of the accident had not yet been determined. The pilot had not mentioned any damage to the aircraft before the crash. The weather was clear. It might well have been due to inexperience. Perhaps the flight engineer had failed to switch over fuel tanks, causing the engines to cut suddenly. There was another factor: it was the pilot's first night solo in a Halifax III.

I thanked the Squadron Commander and left. There was no point in questioning the readiness of the crew for Ops. There was nothing to gain by attaching blame to some young man who couldn't defend himself. They had been training for the best part of two years. Sooner or later you had to turn them loose, I told myself. It was too late for recrimination. They were all dead.

I called a cab to take me to Stonefall Cemetery at Harrogate. It was still raining softly. I got into the front seat with the driver, a short, weathered, middle-aged Yorkshireman. He sized me up pretty quickly.

"Stonefall is it, sir?"

"That's right," I answered.

He drove the short distance to the main gate of the airport, slowed and was waved through by the guard. He stopped at the road, then pulled away.

"Somebody you know, I'm sure," he said.

"My brother," I answered.

"That's too bad, lad. I'm sorry to hear that."

He was quiet for a few minutes, then said contemplatively, "How did it happen? Did the whole crew die"[5]

"All seven were killed. The cause of the crash has not yet been determined. It was just three days ago. They were very inexperienced."

"Do you fly yourself then, lad?" he asked. I was wearing my trench coat and he could not see my wings.

"Yes, I'm a pilot," I said.

"You've flown ops?"

"Yes. Spitfires," I explained.

"Aw well, you know all about it."

He slowed the car a bit. He seemed to be searching for the right words, but he was looking straight ahead, and I wasn't sure whether he was through. He took a big breath, sighed, and the words came somewhat reluctantly. Although it was a long time ago, I quite clearly recall him sitting there behind the wheel. In essence, this is what he said.

"If you don't mind, lad, I'll tell you what I feel about this." His voice was

---

(5)

This was bomber country, and these pragmatic people watched the heavy, four-engined aircraft getting airborne every sunset. It was natural for them to think and speak of aircrew; fighters belonged down south.

gentle, and I had to listen over the slapping of the windshield wipers. I didn't mind listening; I was not in the mood for talking myself.

"It will take a bit of time to get over this," he said. "I'm sure you've lost many friends, but it's different when it's your own kin. It'll take a year, and you musn't rush it. It's got a sort of schedule. But after a year goes by, you'll find it's not so bad. We seem to have a natural ability to adapt to the loss. But it's harder for the women, and it takes somewhat longer. They are closer to t'lads than we are, you know. They have . . . a bad time about it all."

"You seem to have thought quite a bit about this." I looked at him quizzically.

"Aye, that ah have." He lapsed into colloquial speech, a little more at ease now, but still quiet.

"We had three boys, the missus and me. The middle lad was in t' Eighth Army in North Africa. He were killed at El Alamein when Montgomery broke through against Rommel. October 1942 it was."

He stopped for a moment, then continued.

"Our youngest lad was a bomber pilot. An officer, he was, based right here in Yorkshire, about twenty mile away. His Lancaster was shot down by flak over the Ruhr. Direct hit, they told us. Not a chance. One of them thousand bomber raids in June '43. They lost eighty-three aircraft that night."

He stopped talking again for a minute, and looked out the other window of the car, then back to the road.

"Our eldest boy, Jack, was taken prisoner by the Japanese at Hong Kong," he resumed. "Christmas, 1941. Gettin' on t' three years now. We never heard a word from him. I hope he's dead. The Japs aren't civilized about their prisoners, you know. Most of them die slowly of starvation and dysentery. Sooner or later they nearly all die. Jack would be better off dead, I say, although the missus doesn't agree with me. She keeps hoping we'll hear from him someday. Not now, I say."

He sighed again, then gently continued, "We just had the three lads. The war got them all."

A few minutes later he slowed the taxi.

"This is Stonefall." He turned in through the cemetery gates and stopped. "I'll wait for you. You won't want to stay here very long," he said. He seemed to know. Perhaps he was right.
"Thanks," I nodded.

I spoke to the attendant who showed me where to go. This was an official Commonwealth Air Forces Cemetery, and was impeccably kept. Since most aircrew who died never made the return flight, the cemetery was not large. All the graves had headstones, except the recent ones. They had temporary white wooden crosses with the names printed on neatly. I found the boys.

"It's not fair," I thought again, "that these young lads should die on their first trip." But I knew, and had known for a long time, that war was indiscriminate, that there was nothing fair about war at all.

It was time to go. The cabbie was right: I had no wish to stay longer. I went back to the taxi. While waiting for me, the driver had put on an ancient tweed cap. He reached over and opened the door, and we left the cemetery without a word.

Somehow this tough little Yorkshireman's philosophy and fortitude had helped me. It would take a bit of time, he had said, and that was surely true. The war had been unmercifully cruel to him, but it had not broken his spirit. And if he had lost his three sons and was able to carry on with the business of living, I'd better stop feeling sorry for myself. It was time I pulled up my socks.

There was no point in going back to the airport. I was not going to spend my leave here; in fact I didn't know what to do with it. Might as well take the train back to London. I would see the Air Marshal. He might have a job for me.

"Would you take me to the railway station, my friend?" I asked.

"Sure thing, lad," he answered. "Looks like it's goin' to fair up. I think the rain is over."

Flying Officer Carleton G. Kennedy, 434 Squadron RCAF, Yorkshire England. Killed in action, August 30, 1944.

Epilogue

1. The End of the War in Europe.

April 25, 1945: Berlin was surrounded. The Russian army from the east met the American army from the west near Torgau, south of Berlin, on the Elbe River. The British army crossed the Elbe north of Berlin on April 29.

April 30, 1945: Adolf Hitler, in a bunker under the Chancellery in Berlin, committed suicide.

May 1, 1945: The remaining German troops in Berlin surrendered.

May 7, 1945, Rheims: RAF Air Chief Marshal Tedder, General Eisenhower's deputy, Marshal Zhukov of the U.S.S.R., and Field-Marshal Keitel, Chief of German armed forces, signed the document which ended Germany's attempt to dominate the world.

2. Sequel to the War: Philosophy at UNESCO

About 1950, Julian Huxley, the first Director General of the United Nations Educational, Scientific and Cultural Organization, said:

"Man's destiny is to make possible a maximum fulfilment for the greatest number of human beings. This is the only goal at which we must aim."

****

And so the very antithesis of Nazi racial policy prevails at the United Nations. The boys would appreciate that. Jack and Eddie, Timber and Bowie, Geoff and young Tuff, Cecil and David. There was Dal's brother, and Cocky's brother, Rod's brother, and my brother. Goodyear was a Newfie, Gosling from the prairies. And . . . oh, you must have known some of these lads. Their names are on the cenotaphs in all the little towns.

Lament for Humanity, 1944

There was a time of Inhumanity,

When Europe's soul was bared to tyranny,

The innocent asked only to be free,

But rounded up by uniformed decree:

The concentrated smoke of infamy.

With truth suppressed, our frail humanity's

Illusion of not-knowing let it be.

While nothing done to evil seemed unjust

The war evolved; we could not fail the trust

Of Jewish children boxed in railway car

To die at Auschwitz; fault was in their Star.

So will it always be with tyranny:

The tragedy of war's the last resort

When reason fails; there is no higher court.

I.F.K.

APPENDIX 1

Comparative Table of Second World War Aircrew Ranks

Luftwaffe	RAF, RCAF, RAAF, RNZAF	USAF
Officers		
Oberst	Group Captain	Colonel
Oberstleutnant	Wing Commander	Lieutenant Colonel
Major	Squadron Leader	Major
Hauptmann	Flight Lieutenant	Captain
Oberleutnant	Flying Officer	First Lieutenant
Leutnant	Pilot Officer	Second Lieutenant
N.C.O.s		
————	Warrant Officer	Warrant Officer
Oberfeldwebel	Flight Sergeant	Master Sergeant
Feldwebel	Sergeant	Sergeant
Unteroffizier	Corporal	Corporal

APPENDIX 2

Comparison of Luftwaffe and RAF Units

The basic unit of the Luftwaffe was a staffel, which corresponded to an RAF squadron although it was a little smaller than a squadron (eight to twelve aircraft in the air) while larger than a flight. Three staffeln (four later in the war) formed a Gruppe, and three Gruppen formed a Geschwader, the largest individual operational unit. But frequently Gruppen operated independently on different fronts, like RAF Wings of three or four squadrons.

Staffeln and Geschwadern were allocated Arabic numerals, while Gruppen had Roman numerals. In the case of Staffeln and Gruppen, these were placed in front, while Geschwadern had the number behind, and were typically abbreviated:

Jagdgeschwader JG Fighter

Kampfgeschwader KG Bomber

Zerstorergeschwader ZG Heavy Fighter

Schnellkampfgeschwader SKG Fighter-bomber

Nachtjagdgeschwader NJG Night Fighter

Thus III/JG77 referred to III Gruppe of Jagdgeschwader 77.

Reconnaissance units operated as Staffeln only;
eg: H for Heeresaufklarungs (Tactical reconnaissance), thus 2(H)/14 refers to 2 Staffel of Tactical Reconnaissance, Unit 14.

APPENDIX 3

Spitfire Aerodynamics

Sir Morien Morgan, an aerodynamicist who worked on the Spitfire at Farnborough from 1935 to well after the end of the war, has written about the progressive development of higher performance of that aircraft.

"The Spitfire, with her thin wing was able to cope with the greater engine powers and the higher speeds better than any other fighter of her vintage. The thickness-chord ratio at the wing root [the chord is the straight line distance from the leading to the trailing edge of the wing] of the Spitfire was only about .13 percent, compared with 14.8 percent for the Messerschmitt 109 and 16 percent for the Hurricane; even the later Mustang, hailed as a very clean aeroplane, had a 16 percent wing . . . Now on a fattish wing the shock waves begin to form quite early, at about .7 Mach (roughly 500 mph at 20,000 feet, depending on temperature). As the aircraft neared the speed of sound the shock waves got stronger and on those wartime aircraft they would begin to upset the airflow over the wing, effect fore and aft stability, and cause all sorts of unpleasant effects. One way to postpone the Mach effects is to use a swept-back wing [as on jets]; but another is to have a thinner wing and that is why we at Farnborough selected the Spitfire as one of the aircraft for the exploratory work on high speed dives . . . in 1943 . . . Squadron Leader Martindale managed to get a Spitfire XI diving at about .9 Mach . . . I think I am right in saying that this speed was not exceeded until the Americans began their trials with the rocket-powered Bell X1 in 1948 . . .

"Reginald Mitchell's decision to use such a thin wing was not only bold but inspired".   from **"Spitfire at War"** by Alfred Price

Note: re Appendix 3:

Sir Morien Morgan does not deny the slightly faster initial acceleration in a dive of the Me 109 and FW 190. I think his point is that only the Spitfire's wing, among propeller-driven aircraft, allowed a safe diving speed of Mach .85, and this was the recommended limit in the Pilot's Notes for Spitfire IX, XI and XVI, 3rd Edition.

I.F.K

APPENDIX 4
Excerpt from Pilot's Flying Log Book.

DEC 3 SPITFIRE V HNH   SELF   PATROL OVER THE LINES

SUMMARY FOR: SEPT. 15. – DEC. 3. 1943
UNIT NO. 93 SQDN. RAF.
STATION : CAPODICHINO , ITALY

AIRCRAFT   SPITFIRE

TOTAL OPERATIONAL SORTIES : 271

OPERATIONAL HOURS IN ENGLAND   125.30

OPERATIONAL HOURS IN MALTA   119.10

OPERATIONAL HOURS IN SICILY + ITALY 120.40

TOTAL OPERATIONAL HOURS FIRST TOUR 365.20

ENEMY AIRCRAFT DESTROYED : 10
(FIRST TOUR OPS)

CERTIFIED   *A Brawly P/o.*
INTELLIGENCE OFFICER 93 SQDN

GRAND TOTAL [Cols. (1) to (10)]
...7.94...Hrs...10...Mins.   TOTALS CARRIED FORWARD

| | 1.10 | | MY LAST PATROL , FIRST TOUR | | | | |
| 86.30 | | | | | | | |

I Kennedy F/LT.   *Hata* S/LDR D.F.C.
O.C. "A" FLIGHT 93 SQDN.   COMMANDING OFFICER 93 SQDN. RAF.
                           Exceptional as fighter pilot.

POSTED BACK TO BLIGHTY

| 64.00 | 577.40 | 4.50 | 13.20 | 132.20 | 2.00 | | | 44.20 | 21.10 | 12.00 |
| | | | (4) | (5) | (6) | (7) | (8) | (9) | (10) | (11) | (12) | (13) |

APPENDIX 5
RCAF Fighter Squadron Strength
(Ranks in brackets)

Aircrew:

Commanding Officer (Squadron Leader)

"A" Flight Commander
(Flight Lieutenant)
12 pilots
(Commissioned and NCOs)

"B" Flight Commander
(Flight Lieutenant)
12 pilots
(Commissioned and NCOs)

Ground crew:

Engineering Officer (Flying Officer)
Senior N.C.O. (Flight Sergeant)
Second N.C.O. (Sergeant)
N.C.O. Armament (Sergeant)

N.C.O. i/c "A" Flight
(Sergeant)
3 Corporal Fitters or Riggers
12 Fitters (engine mechanics)
12 Riggers (airframe mechanics)
10 Armourers

N.C.O. i/c "B" Flight
(Sergeant)
3 Corporal Fitters or Riggers
12 Fitters
12 Riggers
10 Armourers

Wireless: Corporal and 4 Airmen
Electrical: Corporal and 3 Airmen
Instruments: Corporal and 3 Airmen
Photo: 2 Airmen
Clerical: 3 Airmen
Armament: 2 Corporals

Adjutant (F/O or F/Lt.)

Intelligence Officer (F/O or F/Lt.)

Medical Officer (F/Lt.)

APPENDIX 6

(Normandy)

From: - Officer Commanding, No 13 P.T.C.

To : - Officer Commanding, B. 14 Airfield

Date : - 27th August, 1944.

Ref : - 205/1/P.1

WALKERS BACK

The undermentioned personnel are Walkers Back from enemy territory and are automatically to receive Priority No 1 air transport back to England.

J. 15273. S/Ldr I.F. Kennedy - 401 Squadron.

J. 5478. F/Lt. D.H. Evans - 411 Squadron.

J. 7597. F/Lt. W.R. Tew - 401 Squadron.

J. 6795. F/Lt. A.F. Halcrow - 411 Squadron.

J. 5065. F/Lt. R.C. Cull - 126 Wing.

Warrant Officer for Officer Commanding,

No 13 P.T.C., R.A.F.

References

Grateful acknowledgement is made to the following for permission to reprint previously published material:

1. Bronowski, Jacob (1974). **The Ascent of Man.** Little, Brown and Co. Boston/Toronto. pp. 86,88. Reprinted by permission of the publisher.

2. Donne, John (1624) in **John Donne: Selected Prose** (1987). Edited by Neil Rhodes. Penguin Books, London. p.126 . Reprinted by permission of the publisher.

3. Flower, Desmond, and Reeves, James (1960). **The War 1939-1945,** Cassell and Company, London. pp. 48,124,897,898. Reprinted by permission of the publisher.

4. Hitler, Adolf (1924). **Mein Kampf,** Houghton Miflin Co. Boston (1971). pp. 383, 384. Reprinted by permission of the Estate of Ralph Manheim, Translator, Random House U.K. Ltd. and Hutchinson and Co. Ltd.

5. Keegan, John (1989). **The Second World War.** Penguin Books USA Inc., New York. p.p. 85-86, 101-102, 236-237, 354.Reprinted by permission of Penguin USA and by Sanford J. Greenburger Associates Inc. New York.

6. Price, Alfred (1974). **Spitfire at War.** Ian Allan Ltd., Shepperton, Surrey. pp. 95-97. Reprinted by permission of Dr. Price.

7. Rich, Norman (1973). **Hitler's War Aims**. W.W. Norton and Co., New York. pp. 97-111, 128-131, 204-211. Reprinted by permission of the publisher.

8. Shores, C.F., Ring H., and Hess, W.N. (1975). **Fighters Over Tunisia**. Neville, Spearman Ltd., London. Reprinted by permission of C. F. Shores.

9. Shores, Christopher F. (1992). Private Correspondence. Printed by permission of C. F. Shores.

About the Author

Irving Farmer Kennedy was born in Cumberland, Ontario, just 15 miles from the Peace Tower in Ottawa. In 1940 he joined the RCAF and in 1944 commanded a Spitfire squadron in Normandy.

After the war he stuided medicine at the University of Toronto, graduating with an M.D. in 1950. He completed internship and residency at the Ottawa Civic Hospital, then practiced medicine for 35 years in the Ottawa Valley.

Now retired, Dr. Kennedy lives with his wife Fern in Chickadee Woods near Cumberland. His two daughters and five grandchildren live nearby.

For more copies of

Black Crosses
off my
Wingtip

send $14.95 plus $3.00 for GST, shipping and handling to:

GENERAL STORE PUBLISHING HOUSE
1 Main Street, Burnstown, Ontario
Canada, K0J 1G0
(613) 432-7697 or 1-800-465-6073

OTHER MILITARY TITLES

Black Crosses Off My Wingtip $14.95

The Ridge $14.95

The Memory of All That..$14.95

To the Green Fields Beyond $14.95

The Canadian Peacekeeper..$12.95

Ordinary Heroes..$14.95

Fifty Years After $14.95

One of the Many $14.95

The Surly Bonds of Earth..$12.95

No Time Off for Good Behaviour $14.95

For each copy include $3.00 to cover GST, shipping and handling.
Make cheque or money order payable to:

GENERAL STORE PUBLISHING HOUSE
1 Main Street, Burnstown, Ontario
Canada K0J 1G0